AI SUPER SALES RECRUITER

UNLEASHING AI AND THE POWER OF A VALIDATED PREDICTOR OF SALES PERFORMANCE

JOHN MARSHALL

FREILING
A G E N C Y

Published by Freiling Agency, LLC.

P.O. Box 1264
Warrenton, VA 20188

www.FreilingAgency.com

PB ISBN: 978-1-963701-58-6
E-book ISBN: 978-1-963701-59-3

CONTENTS

YOU'RE NOT JUST HIRING – YOU'RE BUILDING THE FUTURE

Let's be honest—recruiting isn't what it used to be.

The world has changed. So have candidates. So have the stakes.

The old model of flipping through résumés, relying on gut instinct, and hoping for the best? That's done. Today's hiring leaders are under more pressure than ever to move faster, scale smarter, and deliver results—not just hires. The good news? We're better equipped than ever before.

Artificial Intelligence—yes, the buzzword that once felt like science fiction—is now baked into the world of talent acquisition. From sourcing to screening, scheduling to scoring, AI is transforming how we discover, assess, and engage with talent. But here's the catch: AI isn't the star of the show. *You* are.

That's why I wrote *AI Super Recruiter*—not as a love letter to technology but as a field guide for professionals who understand that recruitment is still, at its core, a human business. This book is for recruiters, TA leaders, and business decision-makers who want to lead—not lag—through the next era of hiring.

Why This Book, and Why Now?

Because we're at a tipping point.

Most organizations already have the right building blocks in place: efficient workflows, validated assessments, and performance-based hiring frameworks. Many are already hiring smart—prioritizing potential, aligning with business goals, and focusing on retention. In fact, we already *have* the ideal Talent Acquisition process—it's structured, streamlined, and scientifically validated to predict both performance and retention.

But now, a new question is on the table:

Where Does AI Fit In—and Where Doesn't It?

That's what this book will explore. *AI Super Recruiter* will walk you through the modern TA process stage-by-stage, highlighting where AI adds the most value, where it still falls short, and how to strike the right balance between automation and human insight.

This book is especially critical for organizations with high-volume or continuous-flow recruiting—where hiring never really stops, and every decision directly impacts growth, profitability, and culture. Fast-scaling startups, franchise systems, contact centers, and insurance firms know this better than anyone. And if you're hiring for sales, the pressure is even greater. The cost of hiring the wrong person in a performance-critical role can be enormous.

But when done, right? The payoff is just as big.

AI, when layered onto a proven process, can be a game changer—helping you reduce time-to-fill, improve quality-of-hire, and enhance retention across the board. So, no, this isn't about tossing out everything that works. It's about enhancing what already *does*—with smart, responsible AI integration that works *for* you, not *instead* of you. Because the goal isn't just to hire—it's to hire and retain the *right* people.

Not just faster, but smarter. Not just at scale but with purpose.

You're Not Watching the Revolution— You're Leading It

Whether you're drowning in applications or struggling to find top talent, this book is your roadmap to navigating the new landscape of AI-enabled recruiting. You'll learn how to transform your role from reactive and admin-heavy to proactive, insight-driven, and deeply strategic.

AI won't replace you.

But it will redefine what's possible—if you know how to use it.

So, let's dive in. You're not just about to level up your hiring game. You're becoming an *AI Super Recruiter*. Let's get started.

CHAPTER 1

THE AI RECRUITING REVOLUTION IS ALREADY HERE

In my years working in this field, I've had a front-row seat to some pretty incredible changes. One of the biggest? Watching AI streamline recruiting functions that used to eat up hours, sometimes days, of manual work. It's not just helping out; it's transforming how we operate. Today, AI can do everything from identifying potential candidates using smart, data-driven sourcing strategies to engaging them through AI-powered chat-bots that work around the clock. It doesn't stop there— AI is even screening applications with algorithms that analyze qualifications faster (and often more fairly) than any human ever could.

And now we're reaching a point where even structured interviews—ones based on clear criteria and consistent questions—can be handled, or at least heavily supported, by AI tools. That means what's left for you or the hiring manager is the most human part of the process: the "fit interview." That crucial conversation where you assess not just skills, but cultural alignment, communication style, and the intangible qualities that make someone a great match for your team.

So all of this raises a big, important question: Will AI eventually replace recruiters altogether? Or is it more about reshaping the recruiter's role into something new?

Here's what I think: while there's definitely a future where AI can guide candidates through the early stages of the funnel—qualifying, scheduling, even prepping them for interviews—the role of the recruiter isn't disappearing. It's evolving. Instead of spending time buried in administrative tasks, you'll be leaning into higher-value work. Think: building real relationships with top-tier talent, shaping long-term workforce strategy, and becoming a true advisor to hiring managers.

The shift is already happening. The focus is moving toward strategic thinking, personalized candidate engagement, and developing a deeper, more nuanced understanding of what your organization truly needs, not just for the next hire, but for its future success.

In short, the tools are changing, but the heart of the job—connecting people to meaningful opportunities—is more important than ever. And that heart? It's human, always has been, and always will be.

No matter how powerful AI becomes, no machine can replace the human ability to listen with empathy, read between the lines, or sense the intangible qualities that make someone the right fit—not just for a role, but for a team, a culture, a mission. People still want to be *seen*, *heard*, and *understood*. They want more than just a job—they want to belong, to grow, to thrive. And it takes human intelligence to recognize and nurture that.

That's why *AI Super Recruiter* doesn't treat AI as a replacement for recruiters—it treats it as a powerful partner. AI can process data at lightning speed, eliminate repetitive tasks, and help you make smarter, faster decisions. But you? You bring the vision and the judgment, the ability to connect with another human being on a level that no algorithm can reach. You have both a heart and a brain—and so do the people you're hiring. When you combine that with the strategic use of AI, you're not just filling roles. You're transforming lives and building teams that last.

This book is about mastering that balance. Leveraging the speed and precision of AI while elevating the very human parts of recruiting that can never be automated: trust, intuition, care, and connection. The future belongs to those who can harness both, and you're about to become one of them.

Efficiency vs. Effectiveness: The Heart of AI Recruiting

Two big themes will keep popping up throughout our conversation: efficiency and effectiveness. Right now, most AI in recruiting primarily focuses on efficiency – quickly moving candidates who look good on paper to the next stage, often directly to you or the hiring manager, without really predicting who will succeed.

While this seems to speed things up, it can actually create problems. You might find yourself drowning in candidates who aren't truly qualified, forcing you to spend precious time screening them instead of focusing on the high-quality candidates who could be perfect for the role.

Here's the reality: top talent doesn't stay on the market very long. If you don't engage these high-potential individuals quickly, you'll lose them to competitors. Did you know that 72% of candidates lose interest if they don't hear back within 10 business days? As a result, many companies end up selecting from a pool of average candidates, even though they initially attracted some stellar applicants. Our research suggests many companies only hire 5-15% of the high-quality candidates they initially attract. This inefficient process contributes to burnout among recruiters and hiring managers who waste valuable time sifting through unsuitable profiles.

The real power of AI in recruitment comes from its ability to help you hire more quality candidates. This means shifting toward automating the initial selection steps with predictive tools, so you can focus on engaging and securing top talent. While AI is great at efficiently screening out unsuitable candidates, achieving true effectiveness – consistently identifying and hiring the best people – requires an integrated selection process grounded in data and predictive analytics. I call this "responsible AI."

It's also important to understand that AI isn't the star of the show—it's the value-add. It's the tool that, when plugged in thoughtfully, can take what you're already doing well and make it better, faster, and more efficient.

Think of it like power steering in a car. You're still the one driving. You're still making the turns, navigating the road, choosing the destination. But AI makes it smoother. It removes the friction. It allows you to go further with less effort and greater precision.

The smartest organizations aren't replacing recruiters with AI—they're augmenting their teams with it. They're plugging it in at key points in the process: to speed up sourcing, reduce unconscious bias in screening, automate follow-ups, and analyze patterns that lead to better hiring decisions. It's not about handing over the wheel. It's about giving recruiters more visibility, more insight, and more time to do what only humans can do—build trust, make nuanced decisions, and close with empathy and confidence.

We can help you identify exactly where to apply AI for maximum return on investment—not just in dollars, but in time, quality of hire, and retention. So we'll look at where AI gives you leverage and where human intelligence must stay firmly in the driver's seat. When you strike that balance, you don't just fill roles—you build systems that scale, cultures that thrive, and teams that stick around.

Understanding the Ideal Recruitment Process

Before we dive into how AI is revolutionizing hiring, it's important to take a step back and understand what an ideal talent acquisition process looks like without AI. Think of it as setting the baseline, because only by appreciating the existing best practice structure can we truly grasp how AI enhances and elevates each part of it. All our existing clients have an automated recruiting process that allows candidates to explore and apply for career opportunities from anywhere in the world at any time.

At its core, an effective recruitment process is a structured journey designed to attract, screen, select, hire, and retain top performers.. And while companies may tweak the details based on industry or size, most successful hiring frameworks follow five key stages: including an ongoing validation process that tracks performance and retention data and assesses the effectiveness of each stage at predicting future success, and provides insights and analytics to continuously improve the process.

1. Defining the Ideal Candidate Profile (ICP)

This is where it all begins. Before any job post goes live or outreach begins, the most strategic recruiters spend time getting crystal clear on what a top performer actually looks like. That means identifying not just the obvious skills or credentials, but the deeper competencies, personality traits, and behavioral patterns that tend to predict success within your organization.

This often involves studying your current team, especially the standouts, and comparing what they do differently compared to average or underperforming employees. It's a mix of qualitative insight and, in some cases, quantitative analysis. A well-defined ICP becomes a kind of compass that guides the entire process. The results are significant: Studies show that getting this right can increase the number of high-quality candidates entering your system by up to 300%.

This is referred to as a benchmark study that not only defines the ICP but also provides an ROI if an organization can hire more top-performing candidates and replace the existing current low performers. For example, in sales, most organizations have about 66% of their current group performing at an average level, and about 17% AT A below-average level, AND 17% AT AN above-average level. Replacing the low performers with high performers not only increases the top-line sales but also increases retention and reduces turnover costs, resulting in an exponential increase in profitability. This bridges the gap between HR and IT, who are focused on cost control, efficiency, and risk management (ie, Process), and the CFO, DRO, and Sales leaders, who are focused on results (ie, effectiveness)

2. Attracting and Sourcing

Once you know who you're looking for, the next step is going out and finding them—or better yet, drawing them to you. This is where employer branding, targeted job posts, sourcing strategies, and networking all come into play. You might use platforms like LinkedIn, employee referrals, job boards, or niche communities—whatever works best for the role.

It's not just about visibility, though. It's about resonance. Are you speaking directly to the people you want to attract? Are you showing them why your company is worth their attention?

Super Recruiters and Recruiting Cultures rely on both warm and cold source strategies. Internet and digital marketing of careers are typically cold sources; warm source strategies include both nominators and Centers of Influence (CIOs). Nominators are employees of a company who refer family, friends, neighbors, fellow club members, etc., when they learn about an internal career opportunity, and then refer others in their networks to the opportunities.

COI's are external to the company but a member of the community. A COI might be a local retailer who learns about a career opportunity from a customer and then shares the opportunity with other customers. A COI could be a minor league coach who talks to parents before and after practice and might learn about a career opportunity and share it with other parents and their networks. The type of COIs is endless, professors, influencers, etc.

The benefit of warm source recruiting is that the network is exclusive to the company, whereas all cold source strategies are available to everyone. From our data, the percentage of quality candidates from warm sources is much higher than from cold sources. The role of the Super Recruiter is to make all internal employees aware of opportunities and develop a group of knowledgeable COIs who are aware of the opportunity and how to access the pipeline. Ideally, the recruiter tracks the effectiveness of all referrals and reinforces the referral process, which could be a small gift card, a simple thank you, or even money. Reinforcement theory is simple: if you want a behavior to recur, reinforce it.

NOTE: AI can identify and track referrals, but it can't create the human network

3. Screening and Engaging

This is where the real narrowing down begins. You've got candidates coming in, and now it's time to sort through them. Screening helps you filter out the ones who clearly don't meet your must-haves, and engagement is about beginning those early conversations with the ones who do.

This phase can include reviewing résumés, conducting phone screens, psychometric screening tools, and setting up initial interviews. But more than that, it's about making candidates feel seen, respected, and genuinely excited to move forward.

Current screening best practices separate pre-screening and creating biographic scorecards rather than resumes to screen candidates. Pre-screen character-istics are essential knock-out factors such as language requirements, specific educational requirements like C+ programming courses, if hospitality, maybe 18 years of age, legally eligible to work, but any knock-outs must be nondiscriminatory and job-related, and are basically admission tickets to be considered for the screening process. NOTE: They are not yet considered a candidate.

Biographic scorecards, rather than resumes, are devel-oped from the validation process. Rather than evaluating an entire resume (which is a marketing document), the scorecard evaluates simply the factors that predict job performance. For example, in sales, a scorecard might include warm source (the #1 predictor), previous sales experience, currently employed, currently working >50 hours per week, career progression, natural market (if competitive sales), etc. This saves both the recruiter and candidate time and effectively identifies top-quality candidates who receive the green light to proceed to the selection process. They are now consid-ered a candidate.

4. Selection

The Selection Step is the number 1 predictor of future performance, and the paradigm shifts from deselecting candidates and looking for negatives to selecting the best and looking for positives. At this stage in the recruiting process, the focus has been on efficiency, and the focus now shifts to effectiveness. The ideal Selection system includes both Art and Science. Art is the human element, and Science can be the AI component.,

Predicting Performance is based on the following equation:

Talent is the main predictor of performance and has two major components:

- ***Potential DNA*** that cannot be trained, coached, or created through experience. Potential/DNA is the raw ability that sets our limits for performance.

- ***Skills, competencies, and knowledge*** can be developed through training, coaching, and experience.

The underlining foundation for predicting future performance is set by our potential. It is only through effective training, coaching, and experience that potential becomes performance. Therefore, training skills and competencies and through experience, we can unlock our potential and subsequently our performance.

Even with the assistance of AI, companies run the risk of missing the big picture. AI cannot create potential but it can help identify the key components of potential. Through strategies such as 360's and structured interviewing, we can assess current skills and competencies. Only with these insights can we then create targeted development plans to maximize potential and performance.

In any population, the majority, 66%, falls in the average category.

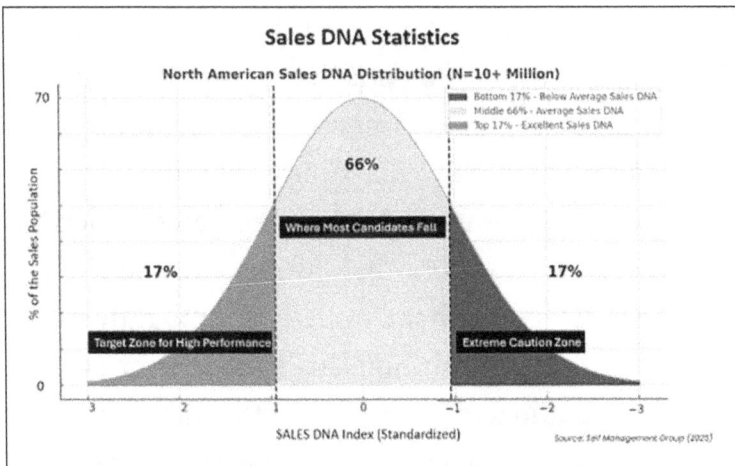

Sales DNA Statistics

North American Sales DNA Distribution (N=10+ Million)

Bottom 17% - Below Average Sales DNA
Middle 66% - Average Sales DNA
Top 17% - Excellent Sales DNA

66%

Where Most Candidates Fall

17%   17%

Target Zone for High Performance   Extreme Caution Zone

% of the Sales Population

SALES DNA Index (Standardized)

Source: Self Management Group (2025)

Therefore, unless Talent Acquisition (TA) prioritises potential, it will be randomly distributed among the normal population. No matter how many resources are invested in individuals with average potential, the performance will be at best average or mediocre. Our research shows that the biggest waste of resources stems from attempting to develop individuals who simply do not have the potential to perform at the highest level. We label these as Talent Traps.

If high potential = high performance, then low potential = low performance

The earlier that potential can be identified, the earlier we can focus on the 17% rather than the 83%. Effective screening strategies eliminate the bottom 17%, while the Selection process identifies the top 17%. With the introduction of AI and advances in technology to automate the TA process, companies have inadvertently increased the volume of average candidates, which has overwhelmed recruiters and hiring managers. They have been forced to filter through the 83% rather than the 17%, leading to hiring a high number of average potential candidates. As a result, the candidates are given to trainers and coaches, forcing the trainers and coaches to invest substantial resources for average to marginal returns.

The **POP**™ identifies *SALES DNA* early in the hiring process, empowering recruiters to zero in on top-quality candidates with high potential. This means hiring managers, trainers, and coaches can focus their time and energy on developing the right people—those who are built to perform. Everyone wins. Recruiters deliver quality, trainers and coaches see a higher return on their efforts, and organizations build high-performing sales teams with precision.

Our clients already excel at building skills and competencies—now they're using the **POP**™ to unlock true potential. Instead of falling into the blame game of underperformance, we help create a sales culture rooted in science, driven by quality, and focused on results. That's the power of selection.

The Sales DNA creates a Predictor Score or algorithm that, for competitive selling, is weighted 50% for will the candidate prospect, 35% for whether they will close, and 15% for whether they fit (which is the main predictor of retention). In other words, if a new sales representative prospects on a daily basis, they will survive. If they prospect consistently and are effective closers; they will excel, and if they fit, they will excel and stay. The algorithm varies by the type of sale, and each of our clients has a custom model.

5. Hiring and Retaining

The Selection process has now identified your best candidate(s), and it is now the responsibility of either the recruiter or the hiring manager to close the sale and hire the best candidate. Remember, top-quality candidates have options, and the career decision is a reciprocal decision. Many recruiters are not trained on how to position or sell the career, or how to use the information collected through the recruiting process to hire the best quality. They often assume that the candidate will automatically take the career if it is offered and do what we call a features sell rather than a benefits sell. In other words, they sell quantitative aspects of the career, such as income, office, etc., rather than on both the quantative and the qualitative aspects that are important to the candidate, such as career progression, growth opportunities, reporting channels, and independence. It is essential to ask the candidate what is important to them and what the characteristics of their ideal career are, which will provide the information to the recruiter to present the career opportunity.

You've made your choice. But the journey doesn't end with a signed offer letter. A great recruitment process flows right into a thoughtful onboarding experience and long-term retention strategy. That includes things like setting clear expectations, building early momentum, checking in often, and giving new hires the support they need to thrive.

Retention starts during recruiting. Candidates want to feel that your company cares about their growth, not just filling a seat. The more intentional you are here, the more likely you are to keep the great people you worked so hard to find. Keeping top performers is called effective retention. There can be a significant gap between Retention and Effective Retention. For example, to simply improve retention, hire dependable, loyal candidates, and create a non-performance-based country club corporate environment, you will have amazing retention, but you might find that your top performers (who we call Golden Eagles) might fly away, and you will have a major performance problem.

There are two major steps to retention: 1) building survival habits and 2) growth, results, and managing success through coaching and corporate support. A consistent finding of research is that most top organizations and coaches know how to train the sales process and sales skills and provide the expertise to continually grow "trainable" talent. However, the major reason sales candidates don't survive or perform well is that the new sales candidate doesn't initiate the sales process through prospecting or business development activity to utilize all the training and skill development. In other words, they "CAN" do the job but don't make the necessary daily commitments to create basic habits to ensure they survive. In all sales organizations, when we ask what differentiates the successful from the unsuccessful, it is always an effort or work habit issue. A unique aspect of our approach to training and coaching is helping new candidates develop basic survival habits. We often ask coaches and leaders, "Is it possible to work hard every day and fail as a sales representative in your company"? The answer is "yes, but it would be difficult".

One of my most interesting consulting experiences was with a large financial services organization that had a two-month, extensive head office training program for new recruits. The program was amazing and included product knowledge, sales process, role play, development of recruits, etc. We asked the sales leaders why reps were failing with such an extensive training program. The answer was "they don't see enough potential clients to utilize the training". We asked how much time in the training program do you dedicate to developing prospecting or business development activities. The answer was that we " don't have time in the training program". The problem was further exacerbated by requiring all new representatives who were not performing up to the standard within three months to undergo an additional one-month head office special training program to help solve the performance problem. Again, the focus of the program was the development of skills and the sales process. You can guess the impact of the additional training, as the focus was on HOW to do the job and not addressing the real issue of "WILL" they do the job. The corporate culture was unconsciously reinforcing individuals for not working hard and creating a "nonperformance corporate culture," often at the expense of the individuals who were working hard and performing. It is a waste of resources and money training a "WILL" issue with a "CAN" approach.

The first step of retention is building in basic survival habits that will give coaches the opportunity to "coach" rather than "coax". The role of coaches is to turn effort into results and most are extremely skilled at coaching. However, dealing with attitudinal or effort issues is much more difficult, as coaches are now required to track or replace habit patterns that are ingrained through years of reinforcement and experience.

Coaxing is attempting to motivate individuals to work hard and develop new, successful habits. This, of course, brings us back to the selection process and the focus of the structured interview to assess the habit patterns of candidates in the pre-higher stage of talent acquisition. Our years of research have demonstrated that new candidates fail because they lack consistent effort. Many coaches waste time with them because they intrinsically lack a strong work ethic.

VALIDATION

The hurdles or roadblocks to performing an effective validation process are typically internal to most organizations. Predictive validation requires data and measurement of each of the five steps at both an input and output level. Attempting to get data on performance and retention is either unavailable or deemed inaccessible because of privacy and confidentiality factors, or the fear of the results of the study. The major goal of a validation study is 1) to determine what factors predict performance and retention, and 2) how well the factors predict.

It is important to ask the right normative question of "how well" rather than the ipsative question "is it working or is it valid". Asking the ipsative question often results in the difference between data and strategy. We have experienced many organizations that have internal data scientists and data analysts who collect data and provide statistical analysis of the data. As statisticians, we enjoy large sample sizes, which often results in statistically significant findings because the power of inferential, parametric statistics rises more quickly than sample size. The result can be a statistically significant finding that has no practical applications. However, identifying what factors in each of the five steps are predictive and developing a customized prediction algorithm can improve the predictability of the algorithm by simply weighing the factors that predict more heavily in the model without taking any additional actionable steps. The statistical analysis can also help streamline the talent acquisition and management process by implementing factors that are either non-predictive or, in some instances, interfering with the prediction model and are negatively correlated to performance. The benefits of streamlining the process improves many factors, such as candidate and recruiter experience. Why collect data from candidates at any stage of the process if it is not predictive? Why screen candidates on specific skills, experience, and competencies if they are not predictive?

VALIDATION (CONTINUOUS IMPROVEMENT)

Validation is the most important and most overlooked aspect of an effective recruiting process. Most processes stop at hiring as the criterion for the evaluation of the recruiting system, which simply maintains the status quo of both current Performance and Retention rates. The key to improving both performance and retention is to be accountable and check how predictive your selection stage was at actually predicting the future and identifying what aspects of each stage are predictive. What are the best sources for attracting top performers, which then provide insights and strategy to focus all your resources on those sources to increase the flow of quality candidates and maximize the ROI on your sourcing strategies?

What factors in your screening process are predicting top performance, and how do you weight the predictive factors more heavily in your screening algorithm, and help set the ideal scorecard or screen to adjust the quality of candidates that get green-lighted to your Selection process.

Continue to improve your Selection Process by leveraging all the components that are predictive and eliminating factors that are not predicting.

Provide performance feedback to your recruiters and hiring managers on what factors are predicting and the effectiveness of their decision making in predicting future performance especially their assessment of the fit to the role, manager and corporate culture.

In other words validation provides feedback on the effectiveness of each stage of the process, improves efficiency by only collecting relevant, predictive information, adapts to changes in the job market, creates the analytics for continuous improvement and maximizes the investment of recruiting resources.

The hurdles or roadblocks to performing an effective validation process are typically internal to most organizations. Predictive validation requires data and measurement of each of the five steps at both an input and output level. Attempting to get data on performance and retention is either unavailable or deemed inaccessible because of privacy and confidentiality factors, or the fear of the results of the study. The major goal of a validation study is 1) to determine what factors predict performance and retention, and 2) how well the factors predict.

Now that we've mapped out the traditional, ideal-state process, here's where it gets exciting: AI doesn't just plug into this framework—it supercharges it. From predictive analytics to automated outreach to intelligent screening tools, AI can improve every stage of this journey, making it faster, more accurate, and more human-centered at the same time.

Let's take a closer look at how AI enhances each step of the recruitment lifecycle.

How AI Revolutionizes Candidate Attraction and Sourcing

AI is transforming how we attract and source talent in ways that were almost unimaginable just a few years ago. Instead of manually scouring LinkedIn, job boards, or niche industry sites, today's AI-powered sourcing tools can do the heavy lifting for you—automatically identifying, screening, and even reaching out to potential candidates across a wide range of online platforms.

These tools operate with incredible speed and precision. They comb through social media profiles, job board activity, personal websites, and professional communities, searching for individuals whose skills, competencies, and work experience match the criteria you've set. Once the match is made, they can invite these candidates to apply through your applicant tracking system (ATS)—whether that's Workday, Greenhouse, Talent Nest AI, or any number of other platforms.

And it works. Recruiters who once spent hours sourcing a single shortlist can now generate strong candidate pipelines in a fraction of the time. The efficiency is a game-changer, especially for high-volume hiring or hard-to-fill roles.

But with that efficiency comes a new set of challenges— ones we can't afford to ignore.

For one, the rise of AI-powered résumé builders has made it easier than ever for candidates to tailor their applications to game the system. These tools don't just help with formatting—they optimize language and keywords to appeal directly to applicant-scanning algorithms. On the surface, that sounds like a win for candidates. However, it also creates a risk for recruiters. When applications are designed more for machines than for humans, the result can be a flood of résumés that look perfect on paper but may not reflect the reality of someone's skills or experience.

In fact, it's estimated that roughly 73% of online résumés include some level of embellishment. That doesn't necessarily mean candidates are being dishonest—it often means they're under pressure to "speak the language" of the algorithm. But it creates a disconnect. AI sourcing tends to prioritize keyword matches and structured data, which means that truly talented individuals who describe their work differently, or who don't optimize their profiles for the algorithm, can get overlooked.

Conversely, those who know how to "speak AI" may rise to the top of your list, even if they're not the most qualified in real life.

There's also a bigger-picture concern: when AI sourcing tools rely heavily on historical hiring data or keyword trends, they can reinforce existing biases. If your past hiring patterns favored certain schools, roles, or even word choices, the AI might prioritize those again, making it harder to build diverse, forward-looking teams.

So while AI is absolutely revolutionizing sourcing, it's not a magic wand. It's a powerful tool—but like any tool, it needs human oversight, strategic thinking, and a clear understanding of both its strengths and its limitations.

As we explore how AI enhances other stages of the recruitment process, we'll keep returning to this idea: the best results come from collaboration between smart technology and thoughtful humans.

AI Chatbots: Revolutionizing Screening and Engagement

Once candidates have been sourced, the next stage in the recruitment journey is screening and engagement, and this is where AI starts to shine in a differFent way. Enter the AI-powered chatbot.

These intelligent assistants, offered by companies like Senseloaf and others, are designed to interact with candidates in real time, often from the moment they land on your careers page or click through a job ad. They can greet candidates, answer basic questions about the role, provide details about the company culture, and—most importantly—initiate the early stages of screening.

These chatbots aren't just conversational gimmicks. They're built to ask targeted, job-specific questions about experience, education, certifications, work preferences, and even long-term career goals. All of this happens in a way that feels natural and accessible to the candidate, often through mobile-friendly chat interfaces that mimic texting or instant messaging.

And the benefit is clear: instead of waiting for a recruiter to find time to schedule a phone screen, candidates can engage instantly, any time of day. For recruiters, this means a faster, more consistent flow of qualified leads moving through the pipeline with minimal manual effort.

But here's the thing—and it's an important distinction that often gets overlooked: what these chatbots are doing is screening, not selecting.

Their primary function is to eliminate—deselect—the candidates who clearly don't meet the minimum criteria. They're great at filtering out those who lack the required experience, credentials, or job eligibility. In other words, they help reduce the noise so recruiters aren't overwhelmed with applications that don't stand a chance.

However, that still leaves a large group of candidates who do meet the minimum threshold. And within that group, you'll often find a wide range of talent, from just barely qualified to truly exceptional. The AI can tell you who's "not a bad fit," but it can't (yet) tell you who's the best possible fit.

That's where human judgment—and a strong, thoughtful selection process—still matter deeply.

Think of it this way: AI screening can help you clear the rubble, but it doesn't necessarily find the gold. It narrows the funnel, but it doesn't shine a spotlight on the hidden gems within that narrowed pool. And if your team isn't prepared to dig deeper—through structured interviews, performance tasks, or deeper conversations—you risk missing out on top talent that simply didn't trigger the right chatbot signals.

So while AI screening tools are an invaluable asset in saving time and streamlining engagement, they aren't a replacement for meaningful candidate evaluation. They're step one—a powerful filter—but they still require a strong, human-driven selection strategy to identify the "pieces of gold" from among the "not unsuitable."

In the next section, we'll talk about how AI can help with that next step: actual candidate selection—and the promise (and limits) of using data to predict success.

Responsible AI: Combining Efficiency with Effectiveness

This is where things start to get truly strategic—and where integrating predictive analytics with a validated assessment methodology becomes essential. Up to this point, AI has helped you attract candidates, engage them, and screen out those who clearly don't meet the basic requirements. But how do you separate the good from the great? How do you identify which of your remaining candidates are likely to become top performers, rather than just check the boxes on a résumé?

That's where my approach, which I call "responsible AI," comes into play. It's a philosophy and a process that combines the best of both worlds: AI's speed and automation capabilities with the accuracy and insight of evidence-based predictive models.

One of the core tools I recommend for this stage is the POP™ (Predictor of Performance) Assessment. This isn't just another personality quiz or generic skills test.

It's a scientifically validated tool designed to evaluate a candidate's inherent potential—the qualities and traits that aren't easily teachable but are critical for long-term job success.

Think of it this way: skills can be trained, but things like resilience, problem-solving instinct, emotional intelligence, and motivational drive? Those are harder to develop after the hire. The POP Assessment zeroes in on these deeper attributes, giving you insight into how a candidate is likely to perform, grow, and adapt in your specific organizational context.

By integrating tools like this into your early selection process, you create a smarter system that does more than just screen out the wrong candidates—it actively identifies and prioritizes the right ones. You're not just avoiding bad hires; you're proactively surfacing great ones.

And here's the real payoff: efficiency and effectiveness.

Instead of spending your time sifting through a sea of candidates who look good on paper but may not have what it takes in practice, you're working with a much more refined pool. These are individuals who have already demonstrated the potential to thrive. So now, your time and energy can go into what you do best—having meaningful, high-impact conversations.

You can focus on getting to know these top candidates as people. You can tailor your pitch, sell the opportunity more effectively, and build a real connection that helps close top talent. And because you're not spread thin trying to evaluate everyone, your interviews become deeper, more strategic, and ultimately more successful.

In short, responsible AI shifts your role from gatekeeper to strategic partner. You're no longer bogged down in paperwork and guesswork—you're leading the charge with insight, precision, and purpose.

And that's what the future of recruiting is all about.

The Art and Science of Selection

I view the selection process through the lens of art and science. The science component includes objective, data-driven aspects like validated psychometric assessments and structured interviews that evaluate competencies and past behaviors (which strongly predict future behavior). AI can effectively deliver and evaluate structured interviews, further automating this scientific aspect.

The art component lies in the fit interview – assessing cultural alignment, team dynamics, and overall organizational fit. While AI is evolving, the nuanced human judgment required for evaluating fit remains critical for you and hiring managers.

Additionally, AI can streamline candidate scheduling, automating the time-consuming process of coordinating interviews. By integrating AI for sourcing, screening, automated selection, and scheduling, you can achieve not only faster hiring but, more importantly, hire the best talent faster.

Benefits for Everyone Involved

What makes this integrated, AI-supported recruitment strategy so powerful isn't just the technology—it's the fact that it delivers real, tangible benefits to everyone involved in the hiring process. When you combine AI-powered engagement, predictive assessments, and automation with thoughtful human decision-making, the experience improves across the board.

For Candidates

Let's start with the people at the heart of the process: your candidates. In a traditional hiring journey, long delays, poor communication, and vague feedback can leave them feeling lost or overlooked. But with AI-driven tools—like chatbots for engagement and assessments that provide clear, actionable insights—candidates enjoy a smoother, more transparent experience from day one.

They're able to interact with your brand on their own schedule, receive quick responses to their questions, and gain clarity on where they stand. And when assessments are part of the process, many candidates walk away with useful information about their own strengths, motivations, and career fit—something they can carry with them, whether or not they get the job. The process feels less like a black hole and more like a meaningful exchange. It is an excellent way to say thank you for taking the time to apply for a position at your company, and maybe they might refer others to your company and career opportunities.

For You, the Recruiter

As a recruiter, the shift is game-changing. You're no longer drowning in busywork—manually screening résumés, scheduling interviews, or chasing down hiring managers for feedback. Instead, you get to focus on what really drives success: engaging with top-tier candidates, selling your organization in a compelling and personalized way, and offering strategic guidance to hiring teams.

You also gain access to richer data. Predictive assessments and AI analytics give you insights into not just who a candidate is, but how they're likely to perform, fit in, and grow. This makes your recommendations stronger, your decisions more defensible, and your impact more visible across the organization.

For Hiring Leaders

Your hiring managers are busy people, and often, they just want to find the right person as efficiently as possible. With this integrated approach, they can.

Automated scheduling tools remove the back-and-forth of coordinating interviews. Pre-screened, high-potential candidates land on their desk ready to impress. And best of all, assessment data gives them concrete, consistent information about each finalist—so they're not making choices based on gut instinct alone.

This not only speeds up hiring but improves decision quality. Hiring managers feel more confident, more involved, and more supported by the process.

For the Organization

Zooming out, the organization as a whole reaps serious rewards.

With AI handling repetitive tasks and helping you move faster, your time-to-hire can decrease by up to 10x—a critical advantage in competitive talent markets. You'll also see a threefold increase in the number of quality candidates entering the funnel because your sourcing and screening become sharper and more targeted.

Drop-off rates go down because candidates feel informed and engaged. Retention goes up because you're making better matches. Overall performance improves because you're consistently hiring people who are well-suited for the roles and ready to succeed.

In short, this isn't just about making recruiting easier. It's about making it better—more human, more strategic, and more impactful for everyone involved.

The Foundation of Success: The Ideal Candidate Profile

Underpinning this approach is the Ideal Candidate Profile (ICP), which ensures AI algorithms target individuals who best fit your specific organization and role. The AI algorithms are loaded with ICP attributes, leading to higher-quality candidates.

The Performance Equation (Talent × Habits × Opportunity) helps understand key success predictors:

- **Talent** includes inherent potential/DNA (measured by psychometric assessments) and trainable skills/experience (evaluated through screening).

- **Habits** refer to attitude and effort, assessed through structured interviews.

- **Opportunity** considers the fit between the candidate and the career, work environment, culture, and manager, and is assessed through unstructured interviews.

High performance and retention happen when there's strong alignment across all three factors.

Addressing AI's Potential Pitfalls

We need to acknowledge the potential dangers of AI in recruiting, particularly regarding bias and discrimination. If AI algorithms train on historical data reflecting existing biases, they can perpetuate and amplify these biases, negatively affecting certain groups. Amazon once had to drop an AI recruiting tool due to discriminatory outcomes, highlighting the importance of careful design and continuous monitoring for bias-free, ethical AI hiring.

Validation and continuous improvement are essential for successful AI-powered recruitment. Regularly tracking performance and retention of AI-assisted hires allows you to assess effectiveness and identify areas for refinement. This iterative approach ensures

AI remains predictive and continues improving your talent acquisition function.

Throughout the rest of our journey together, we'll explore each aspect in depth, providing practical strategies for effectively implementing AI throughout your recruitment process. By understanding AI's power and limitations, embracing responsible AI principles, and strategically integrating technology with human expertise, you can transform your hiring process, attract and secure top talent, and build a high-performance organization.

Welcome to the era of the AI Super Recruiter!

CHAPTER 2

THE IDEAL TALENT ACQUISITION PROCESS WITHOUT AI

Before we dive into how AI is reshaping the future of talent acquisition, it's important to start with a solid foundation: understanding what a truly effective hiring process looks like without AI. Why? Because by clearly outlining the traditional approach, we'll be able to see—step by step—where AI adds value, fills gaps, and elevates your effectiveness in ways that were previously out of reach.

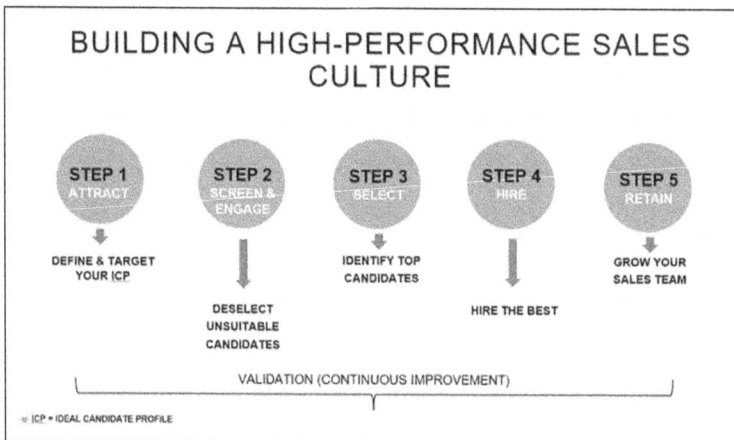

BUILDING A HIGH-PERFORMANCE SALES CULTURE

STEP 1 ATTRACT — DEFINE & TARGET YOUR ICP

STEP 2 SCREEN & ENGAGE — DESELECT UNSUITABLE CANDIDATES

STEP 3 SELECT — IDENTIFY TOP CANDIDATES

STEP 4 HIRE — HIRE THE BEST

STEP 5 RETAIN — GROW YOUR SALES TEAM

VALIDATION (CONTINUOUS IMPROVEMENT)

* ICP = IDEAL CANDIDATE PROFILE

So let's walk through the five key stages of an ideal hiring process. This framework isn't just theoretical—it's practical, proven, and already used by high-performing organizations around the world. It's what successful recruiting looks like before the algorithms and automation step in.

Step 1: Defining the Ideal Candidate Profile (ICP)

This is where it all begins. The cornerstone of any successful hiring strategy is clarity—knowing exactly who you're looking for before you start looking. As I often say, "If you don't know who you're after, you'll probably find somebody else."

This step goes far beyond a generic job description. It's about drilling down into what specific skills, traits, and behaviors consistently lead to success in a particular role within your unique environment. Who are the high performers already on your team? What do they do differently? What patterns emerge when you compare them to those who struggled or left the role early?

One highly effective tactic here is to conduct a benchmark study—a side-by-side comparison of top performers and underperformers. Look at technical competencies, soft skills, motivation styles, and even cultural alignment. The goal is to build a profile that reflects not just what's required, but what leads to excellence.

And it's worth the effort: a well-crafted ICP can increase the number of quality candidates entering your pipeline by up to 300%, simply because you're aligning your outreach and messaging with the right people from the start.

Step 2: Screening to Deselect Unsuitable Candidates

Once your ICP is in place, the next step is screening—a process focused on efficiently eliminating candidates who don't meet your baseline requirements.

Think of it like panning for gold. You're not trying to find the treasure yet—you're just trying to clear out the obvious non-fits so you can spend your time more productively. This typically involves reviewing résumés, scanning for key qualifications, and applying predefined filters like education level, work history, or location.

Without AI, this step often requires long hours and sharp instincts. And while it's critical, it also comes with the risk of overlooking great candidates simply because of time constraints or unconscious bias. Still, the goal here is simple: reduce noise, so you can focus your energy where it counts.

Step 3: Selection to Identify Top Candidates

Now we shift gears—from narrowing the field to actively identifying the stars within it. This is where selection begins: the process of distinguishing between candidates who are simply "qualified" and those who are truly exceptional.

This stage typically includes structured interviews, validated psychometric assessments, case studies, and reference checks. It's also where you, as a recruiter, bring real value—by using your judgment, intuition, and experience to assess more than what's on paper.

You're looking for alignment with your ICP, of course—but also for intangibles like learning agility, emotional intelligence, and cultural fit. And without AI, that means digging deep. It's time-intensive, yes—but absolutely essential for making strong, confident hiring decisions.

Step 4: Hiring the Best

Once you've identified your top candidate(s), it's time to close the deal. And in today's competitive market, this phase is all about speed, clarity, and connection.

The best candidates—especially those who've demonstrated high potential—are rarely on the market for long. A slow or disjointed hiring process can easily cost you a great hire. That's why this stage demands urgency and intentionality.

You, as the recruiter, play a pivotal role here. You're not just delivering the offer—you're selling the opportunity. You're translating what makes your company great into terms that matter to this specific candidate. Why should they choose you over the three other offers on the table? What unique value does your role offer for their career path?

Hiring the right person is about more than filling a seat—it's about closing with conviction and creating a compelling case that brings top talent across the finish line.

Step 5: Retaining Top Performers

Hiring doesn't stop with a signed contract. In fact, that's just the beginning. The final—and often most overlooked—stage of the hiring process is retention. After investing so much effort into finding the right person, the goal is to keep them engaged, growing, and contributing over the long haul.

This means thoughtful onboarding, personalized development plans, regular coaching, and a supportive culture that encourages people to bring their full selves to work. It also means aligning their role with their aspirations—helping them see a future with your organization.

Retention is about more than keeping people—it's about keeping the right people. The high performers. The culture-builders. The folks who make your team better every day. And when you retain top talent, you build momentum—because high-performers attract other high-performers.

When executed with care and clarity, this five-step process forms the backbone of effective hiring, even without AI. But as you've probably noticed, it also includes plenty of opportunities for friction, inefficiency, and human error. That's where AI comes in.

In the chapters ahead, we'll explore how AI can strategically enhance each of these five stages—helping you work smarter, make better decisions, and build world-class teams faster and more effectively than ever before.

CHAPTER 3

AI-POWERED ATTRACTION AND SOURCING STRATEGIES

Now that we've established what a strong, traditional talent acquisition process looks like, let's dive into how AI is transforming the early stages, particularly attraction and sourcing. These are the phases where you're casting your net and looking to bring potential candidates into your funnel. And this is exactly where AI can make an immediate, measurable impact.

Modern AI tools don't just help you move faster—they enable you to be more precise, more responsive, and more strategic. But like any powerful tool, how you use it makes all the difference.

Leveraging AI for Candidate Identification

At its core, AI is a pattern-recognition engine. It can scan massive volumes of data across countless digital channels and identify patterns that point to candidates

AI SUPER SALES RECRUITER   JOHN MARSHALL

who match your needs. Instead of manually searching, you can now rely on smart algorithms to do the legwork, working 24/7 and combing through millions of data points in seconds.

Here's where AI can search for talent:

Social Media Platforms

Platforms like LinkedIn, Facebook, and even Twitter/X contain a treasure trove of public professional information. AI can analyze profiles, activity, and connections to identify potential candidates with relevant backgrounds and expertise.

Job Boards and Aggregators

AI sourcing tools can crawl sites like Indeed, Monster, ZipRecruiter, and niche boards to find résumés, portfolios, and job-seeking signals—like people recently updating their profiles or showing interest in similar roles.

Company Career Sites

Some advanced AI systems can also monitor traffic on your own careers page, analyzing candidate behavior (what jobs they viewed, how long they stayed, which pages they clicked) to help flag potential strong matches—even before they apply.

What's powerful here is that you can customize your AI tools to prioritize specific criteria: skills, certifications, job titles, years of experience, geographic proximity, and more. You're no longer casting a wide, unfocused net—you're tuning your system to find exactly what your team needs. And once a candidate is identified, AI can go one step further by automatically inviting them to your job portal or directly into your Applicant Tracking System (ATS), whether you use Workday, Lever, Talent Nest AI, or another platform.

The Promise—and the Pitfalls— of AI Efficiency

AI's biggest selling point in the sourcing phase is efficiency. It can identify and engage hundreds (even thousands) of candidates faster than a team of recruiters ever could. In theory, this should massively boost your pipeline and give you more talent to work with.

But here's the catch: more isn't always better.

More Volume, Not Always More Quality

If your AI is operating without clear guidance, especially without alignment to a solid Ideal Candidate Profile (ICP), you could end up drowning in applications. Yes, your candidate count will go up, but so will your workload, and much of your time may be spent filtering through people who don't truly fit. This can actually decrease your efficiency if you're not careful.

The Rise of AI-Optimized Résumés

Candidates are getting smarter—and more tech-savvy. With the rise of AI-powered résumé generators, many applicants are now using tools to tailor their résumés specifically to appeal to ATS and sourcing algorithms. While this shows initiative, it can also distort reality. Embellishments are becoming more common, and in some cases, entire résumés are being generated by other algorithms. That makes it harder to gauge someone's actual qualifications just by skimming their résumé.

Estimates suggest that over 70% of online résumés contain some form of embellishment. The result? Your AI may be matching based on keywords and formatting rather than true fit or substance.

The Quantity Trap

Just because AI helps you attract more candidates doesn't mean you're any closer to finding the right candidates. In fact, high-quality candidates often have limited patience. If your process feels robotic, impersonal, or slow to respond, they'll move on to your competitors. The takeaway? You need more than just a wide net—you need a sharp, strategic filter.

The Key to Unlocking AI's Full Potential: Targeting the Ideal Candidate Profile (ICP)

This is why your Ideal Candidate Profile (ICP) isn't just a nice-to-have—it's essential. It's the input that determines the quality of your AI's output.

When you align your AI tools with a well-defined ICP, the sourcing process becomes much more focused. Instead of surfacing everyone who happens to have "project manager" in their title, for example, your AI is now prioritizing candidates who match your version of what success looks like in that role—your competencies, your culture, your mission.

What this leads to:

- A Higher Quality Pipeline: You don't just get more résumés—you get more relevant résumés.

- Reduced Workload: You're spending less time sifting through false positives and more time having meaningful conversations with promising candidates.

- Improved Hiring Outcomes: Because you're targeting fit from the very beginning, your interview-to-hire ratio improves—and so does retention.

- AI-Powered Engagement: Keeping Candidates Warm and Interested

Sourcing is only half the story. Once you've attracted candidates, you need to engage them, and AI helps here too.

Chatbots and virtual assistants now play a vital role in the early engagement phase. These aren't clunky, scripted bots from ten years ago. Today's AI chatbots are responsive, natural, and genuinely helpful. Here's what they can do:

- Provide Immediate Responses: No more waiting days for a recruiter to follow up. Chatbots can instantly acknowledge a candidate's interest and begin a conversation.

- Answer FAQs: Candidates often have common questions—about benefits, remote policies, role expectations. AI can handle these at scale.

- Pre-Screen Candidates: Chatbots can ask early-stage questions to assess qualifications, interest level, and availability.

- Personalize the Experience: Smart bots can even address candidates by name, reference past interactions, and guide them through next steps—keeping them engaged and informed.

This automation doesn't just help you manage volume—it also improves the candidate experience, which is becoming a major differentiator in talent acquisition.

The Bottom Line

AI offers tremendous potential to supercharge your attraction and sourcing strategy. But if you want it to actually improve hiring outcomes—not just inflate your numbers—you need to guide it with strategy. That means anchoring everything in a well-defined ICP and coupling AI's reach with smart human judgment.

When used wisely, AI won't just help you find more people—it'll help you find the right people faster. And that's the kind of competitive edge every recruiter wants.

CHAPTER 4

AI CHATBOTS FOR SCREENING, ENGAGEMENT, AND SCHEDULING

Following our discussion of AI-powered attraction and sourcing strategies, let's now explore how AI chatbots handle screening, engagement, and even scheduling. These conversational agents act as intermediaries, interacting with potential hires after they've been attracted to your opportunity.

The Role of AI Chatbots in Your Recruitment Funnel

Once candidates are sourced and invited to apply, AI chatbots play a crucial role in guiding them through the early stages of your recruitment funnel. They act as intelligent front-line assistants—automating essential tasks, maintaining engagement, and beginning the screening process—tasks that would otherwise consume a significant amount of recruiter time.

The first way chatbots add value is through initial engagement and information sharing. As soon as a candidate expresses interest or submits an application, the chatbot can greet them, acknowledge their submission, and answer common questions about the role, your company culture, or the application timeline. This instant feedback keeps candidates engaged and informed, reducing the risk of drop-off during a process that can often feel opaque or slow-moving.

From there, chatbots take on preliminary screening and qualification. You can configure them to ask job-specific questions that probe beyond what's listed on a resume. This might include inquiries about relevant experience, technical skills, certifications, or availability. These early assessments help refine your candidate pool, allowing only those who meet your baseline criteria to move forward, saving you time and effort later in the process.

Equally important, chatbots help maintain candidate interest. Their conversational, interactive nature offers a sense of ongoing communication, even before a recruiter gets involved. This matters because in today's competitive job market, candidates who don't hear back quickly often lose interest or accept other offers. Prompt, AI-powered engagement sends a clear signal that your organization is responsive and values their time.

How AI Chatbots Facilitate Screening

AI chatbots do more than just ask questions—they analyze responses in real time using embedded algorithms designed to identify patterns, keywords, and indicators of suitability. By matching candidate input with predefined role criteria, the chatbot can effectively filter out individuals who clearly do not meet essential requirements. This process of automated de-selection ensures that your attention is directed toward candidates with a higher likelihood of success.

In addition to filtering, chatbots are capable of gathering more detailed insights by asking dynamic follow-up questions based on a candidate's initial responses. This gives you richer context on a candidate's background and skills—before you even review their application—allowing for a more informed next step in the process.

Because chatbots ask the same questions in the same way to every candidate, they also bring a layer of consistency and objectivity to your early-stage screening.

This reduces potential bias, increases fairness, and helps create a level playing field for all applicants.

Integrating Scheduling Capabilities

Beyond screening and engagement, many AI chatbots now include automated interview scheduling, adding even more efficiency to your recruitment process. Once a candidate passes initial screening, the chatbot can offer them a selection of available time slots to schedule an interview directly with you or a hiring manager, without any back-and-forth emails or delays.

This streamlined scheduling functionality not only enhances the candidate experience but also frees up your time for higher-value activities, like building relationships with top candidates, advising hiring teams, or fine-tuning your talent strategy. With administrative tasks off your plate, you can focus on what matters most: making smart, timely hiring decisions that strengthen your organization.

In short, AI chatbots serve as an essential part of a modern recruitment funnel—automating early steps, maintaining momentum, and ensuring that by the time you step in, you're engaging with the candidates who are most likely to succeed.

Benefits of Utilizing AI Chatbots

Integrating AI chatbots into your talent acquisition process can deliver a powerful combination of speed, efficiency, and improved candidate experience—all while freeing up valuable recruiter time. These tools are particularly effective in the early stages of hiring, where high volume and repetitive tasks often slow down progress and drain team resources.

One of the most immediate advantages is a significant increase in efficiency. AI chatbots can automate essential but time-consuming tasks such as initial screening, responding to frequently asked questions, and coordinating interview schedules. By offloading these responsibilities to a virtual assistant, your recruitment process moves faster and becomes more consistent, ensuring no candidate falls through the cracks during those early interactions.

At the same time, chatbots help create a more engaging and responsive candidate experience. Job seekers receive immediate replies, rather than waiting days for a human follow-up, which helps maintain interest and momentum. The conversational interface of a well-designed chatbot feels intuitive and familiar, offering a smoother, less transactional experience that reflects positively on your employer brand.

By managing the initial workload, AI chatbots also contribute to increased productivity for recruiters and hiring managers. With early-stage tasks handled automatically, your team can shift focus to more strategic responsibilities—like building relationships with top candidates, fine-tuning selection processes, or improving employer branding initiatives. This not only drives better results but also reduces the risk of burnout in high-volume hiring environments.

Perhaps most crucially, chatbots contribute to a faster overall time-to-hire. By accelerating candidate screening and interview scheduling, the process becomes more streamlined, allowing you to make quicker decisions and secure top talent before competitors do. In today's competitive job market, speed often makes the difference between a successful hire and a missed opportunity.

Finally, modern AI chatbots offer a surprising degree of personalization. They can address candidates by name, adapt messaging based on specific roles or interests, and even recall past interactions, making the entire process feel more human, even though it's powered by automation.

In short, AI chatbots enhance both the efficiency and quality of your hiring process. They allow you to operate at scale without sacrificing the candidate experience and create the space for your team to focus where human insight matters most.

Considerations for Implementing AI Chatbots

AI chatbots offer clear advantages in streamlining the talent acquisition process, especially when it comes to automating initial engagement and screening. However, to fully realize their potential, organizations must implement them thoughtfully, with attention to both functionality and candidate experience.

A chatbot's effectiveness begins with well-defined screening criteria. The quality of the questions it asks—and the accuracy of the algorithms used to evaluate responses—play a crucial role in determining whether suitable candidates are accurately identified.

This means investing time upfront to carefully design the conversation flow, establish clear benchmarks, and ensure the chatbot reflects your organization's hiring standards.

Equally important is ensuring a positive and natural user experience. While candidates increasingly expect some level of automation during the hiring process, they also expect it to be seamless, intuitive, and respectful of their time. Poorly designed chatbots that feel robotic, repetitive, or confusing can quickly lead to frustration and may even damage your employer brand. Every interaction should feel helpful and human-centered, even when no person is involved.

It's also essential to define the appropriate scope for chatbot interactions. AI chatbots are highly effective for early-stage tasks like answering FAQs, conducting pre-screening, and scheduling interviews. However, more complex evaluations, such as assessing cultural fit, interpersonal dynamics, or long-term motivation, typically require human involvement. Knowing where the chatbot's role ends and where human recruiters should step in helps maintain the quality and integrity of your hiring process.

Another vital consideration is addressing potential algorithmic bias. Like all AI-driven tools, chatbots are only as fair and accurate as the data and logic behind them. To prevent discriminatory outcomes, organizations must regularly monitor chatbot behavior, test for bias, and validate results against real hiring outcomes. This helps ensure the chatbot supports an inclusive and equitable recruiting process.

When implemented strategically, AI chatbots can significantly enhance the efficiency and effectiveness of your recruitment efforts. They automate time-consuming tasks, provide engaging and responsive candidate interactions, and streamline the early stages of the hiring journey. By thoughtfully designing the chatbot experience and closely monitoring its performance, you create a system that not only improves your internal workflows but also delivers a faster, more positive hiring experience, laying the groundwork for a truly high-performing workforce.

CHAPTER 5

AI SCREENING AND CAREER MATCHING ALGORITHMS AND TOOLS

Now that we've seen how AI chatbots can handle early engagement—providing timely responses, answering common questions, and conducting basic screening—it's time to explore what happens next. The real magic of AI in recruitment lies in its ability to go further: screening more deeply and matching more intelligently.

We're now entering a more advanced phase of the recruitment process—one where AI doesn't just engage candidates, but actively helps you evaluate and route them in meaningful, strategic ways.

Moving Beyond Initial Chatbot Screening

While AI chatbots serve as a helpful first line of interaction, flagging candidates who meet basic requirements, the technology doesn't stop there. More sophisticated AI screening tools can dive deeper, analyzing a much broader set of inputs to give you a more complete and nuanced picture of each applicant.

These tools can analyze:

Résumés and Cover Letters

AI algorithms can now parse unstructured text in résumés and cover letters to extract keywords, identify core competencies, and determine a candidate's experience level, educational background, and even communication style.

Online Professional Profiles

Publicly available profiles on LinkedIn, Facebook, Behance, and other platforms offer insights into skills, endorsements, certifications, work history, and even thought leadership activity. AI can synthesize this information at scale to build fuller candidate profiles.

Application Form Data

Responses to application form questions—especially open-ended ones—are no longer ignored or skimmed over. AI can evaluate these for intent, tone, and relevance to job criteria, helping you better understand who's a fit and who isn't.

The result? A cleaner, more manageable list of candidates who have cleared a foundational threshold—people worth taking a closer look at.

The Efficiency vs. Effectiveness Paradox in AI Screening

As we've touched on before, AI's greatest strength is efficiency—its ability to process massive volumes of data faster and more consistently than a human ever could. But speed alone isn't enough.

There's a critical distinction to understand here:

Efficiency is about moving quickly, screening out unqualified candidates by matching them against a predefined list of required attributes. It's largely descriptive: Does the person have the listed skills?

Effectiveness, on the other hand, is about moving smartly—identifying candidates who are not only qualified but also likely to succeed, grow, and stay. This requires a more predictive approach that goes beyond keywords and surface-level traits.

And here's the problem: without a validated, integrated selection step to follow up on AI screening, you can end up trading one kind of overwhelm for another. Instead of manually screening a giant applicant pool, you're now looking at a slightly smaller—but still too broad—pool of "paper-qualified" candidates. That pool may still include plenty of mismatches; even worse, you might miss high-potential individuals who didn't keyword-optimize their application the "right" way.

Career Matching Algorithms: Connecting People to the Right Roles

In addition to helping you screen candidates for a specific position, AI can also assist with career matching—a powerful tool for building internal pipelines, improving the candidate experience, and making better long-term hiring decisions.

Here's how:

Internal Mobility

AI can scan internal employee data—like work history, performance reviews, and development plans—to identify existing employees who may be perfect for current openings. This promotes retention, reduces external recruiting costs, and signals growth opportunities for your people.

Alternative Role Suggestions

Not every candidate will be a perfect match for the role they initially apply for—and that's okay. AI can help redirect them to other open roles where their experience and aspirations might be a better fit. It's a win-win for the candidate and employer.

Personalized Career Pathing

Looking ahead, AI is poised to play a bigger role in helping individuals map out personalized career trajectories within your organization. Based on their skills and interests, the system can suggest development opportunities and likely next steps. This can transform the recruiting process into a long-term talent engagement journey.

Why the Ideal Candidate Profile (ICP) Still Matters

To make all of this work—to turn AI screening from a blunt instrument into a strategic advantage—you need to anchor it in a well-defined Ideal Candidate Profile (ICP).

Your ICP is more than a job description—it's a performance blueprint. It includes the specific traits, competencies, and behaviors that predict success in your environment. By integrating these criteria into your AI tools, you enable the system to filter candidates not just by what they've done, but by how well they're likely to do in your organization.

This alignment turns AI screening into a proactive tool, not just removing unqualified candidates, but spotlighting the right ones.

The Limits of AI: Skill Presence = Skill Depth

One of the common misconceptions around AI screening is that if a candidate lists a skill, they must be good at it. But this is a dangerous assumption.

Today's AI tools can confirm the presence of a skill, but they can't fully assess its quality or depth. Two candidates may both list "project management" on their résumés, but one may have led global teams while the other coordinated a single local event. On paper, they match. In practice, their capabilities could be worlds apart.

That's why human evaluation—and ideally, structured assessments—remain critical. AI can narrow the pool, but only deeper interviews and performance-based evaluations can surface the truly exceptional candidates.

Toward Predictive Selection: The Need for an Automated, Intelligent Process

To truly identify top performers—the ones with the ability to thrive and stay—you need to go beyond screening and build a selection process that is predictive, data-informed, and consistent.

This is where tools like the Selection Rater, which we'll explore in Chapter 5, come in. These systems help you move from reactive hiring to a repeatable, science-backed process that aligns every hire with your organization's long-term goals.

Some of the more advanced AI tools are already inching in this direction by offering candidate ranking features—prioritizing applicants based on how closely they match the job requirements and your ICP. This helps you focus your attention where it matters most—on candidates most likely to succeed.

Final Thoughts: Efficiency Is the Start— Effectiveness Is the Goal

AI-powered screening and career matching can supercharge your recruiting process. They help you move faster, reach more people, and manage complexity at scale. But to truly make them count, you need to go one step further.

You need to strategically align AI with your ICP, build in predictive assessments, and stay focused not just on finding candidates—but on finding the right candidates.

When used responsibly, AI doesn't just make recruiting faster—it makes it smarter, more human, and more aligned with what your business actually needs to succeed.

CHAPTER 6

SELECTION RATER – COMBINING THE ART AND SCIENCE OF SELECTION

Now that we've explored AI-powered screening tools, let's shift our focus to selection—the critical process of identifying the best candidates from those who are merely not unsuitable. I'd like to introduce you to the Selection Rater, a framework that combines the objective power of data and automation with the nuanced judgment of human insight, ultimately leading to more effective and quality hires.

Moving from Screening to Selection: Identifying the "Gold"

As we discussed previously, AI excels at efficient screening, acting as a "panning for gold" mechanism to remove obviously unsuitable candidates. However, your remaining pool still contains candidates ranging from below average to superior. Selection is the process of carefully examining this "ore" to identify the valuable "gold"—individuals with the highest potential for performance and retention.

The Selection Rater provides a structured approach to this critical phase, acknowledging that truly effective hiring requires more than just matching resume keywords. It integrates objective, data-driven assessments with subjective, human-centered evaluations.

The Three Pillars of the Selection Rater

The Selection Rater comprises three key components, each contributing a unique perspective to your overall candidate evaluation:

1. **Psychometric (100% Science - Automated)**: This component forms the foundation, providing an objective and scientifically validated assessment of a candidate's inherent potential. These psychometric assessments evaluate untrainable aspects of talent, often related to cognitive abilities, personality traits, and behavioral tendencies predictive of success in specific roles. Leveraging AI and automation, this stage efficiently assesses many candidates without direct

human interaction. This aligns with using AI for efficiency in initial selection steps, ensuring only those with foundational potential advance.

2. **Structured Interview (Incorporating "50% Art & 50% Science"):** This component refers to a standardized interview conducted by either you or the hiring manager where all candidates are asked the same questions and their responses are scored and tracked for their effectiveness in predicting future performance. The Structured interview is 50% science as it follows a systematic process and 50% Art as it requires the interviewer to score the responses. The structured interview typically includes the core competencies of the company and the specific skills required in a specific role. It also assesses work ethic by asking about attitudinal and behavioral habit patterns. It leverages the "art" of selection or the human aspect of intuition with the attractiveness of AI in following the scientific method.

3. **Fit Interview (Incorporating "100% Art):** This final component specifically focuses on the candidate's fit with the team, hiring manager, corporate culture, and specific role demands... This interview is often left to you or the hiring

manager, further emphasizing the importance of human judgment in evaluating these subjective but critical factors. AI isn't yet capable of accurately assessing this "fit" aspect, which often relies on personal connection and intuition. This aligns with the idea that while AI can automate the "science," the "art" of understanding human nuances remains essential.

Our ongoing research indicates that if the Art and Science are aligned in assessing potential, the accuracy of prediction is significantly more predictive than either component on its own. In other words, they are complementary. If all three components are rated high, the accuracy in performance prediction is over 90%. If only two are high, the accuracy drops to about 66%, and if one is high, it depends on which component, as a validated psychometric assessment will outperform Art because of the Chemistry that sometimes interferes with the evaluation process of humans.

Focusing on the Automated Psychometric Component (100% Science)

Let's focus on the psychometric component, which is now largely automated through AI. These AI-powered assessments provide standardized, bias-free evaluation of candidate potential and subsequently predict performance. By analyzing patterns and correlations in vast datasets of successful and unsuccessful employees, these algorithms predict which candidates possess inherent traits linked to high performance and retention.

The Benefits of Automating the Science of Selection

- **Increased Efficiency**: AI rapidly administers and scores these psychometric assessments at scale, significantly reducing the time and resources required for initial candidate evaluation.

- **Enhanced Objectivity**: Automated assessments minimize potential unconscious biases that can influence human evaluations in traditional screening methods.

- **Improved Predictive Accuracy**: When based on rigorous validation studies, psychometric assessments provide valuable insights into a candidate's success potential, leading to more effective hiring decisions.

- **Focus for You**: By automating this initial, data-driven selection stage, you can focus your time and energy on more strategic, human-centric aspects of the hiring process, such as conducting in-depth interviews with truly promising candidates.

Integrating with the Ideal Candidate Profile (ICP)

The psychometric component's effectiveness is significantly enhanced when aligned with the Ideal Candidate Profile (ICP) developed in your initial talent acquisition stages. By identifying specific inherent traits predictive of success for particular roles within your organization (as defined by the ICP), you can tailor psychometric assessments to identify candidates possessing these crucial qualities. This moves beyond generic assessments to focus on individuals most likely to thrive in your unique context.

The Transition to Human Evaluation: The "Art" of Selection

While the psychometric component provides a powerful, efficient first selection step, remember it represents only one-third of the Selection Rater. The subsequent unstructured and fit interviews are essential for bringing in the "art" of selection. These stages allow deeper understanding of the candidate's experiences, motivations, cultural fit, and interpersonal skills—aspects currently beyond AI's comprehensive capabilities.

By strategically combining the science of automated psychometric assessments with the art of human evaluation in later Selection Rater stages, you can move beyond hiring paper-qualified candidates to identifying and securing top talent who are not only capable but likely to be high performers and long-term contributors. This integrated approach embodies responsible AI recruitment principles, leveraging technology to enhance efficiency and objectivity while preserving the essential human element in crucial hiring decisions.

In the following chapters, we'll explore the Structured Interview (Chapter 7) and the Fit Interview (Chapter 8), further examining how to effectively integrate the "art" and "science" of selection to maximize hiring success in the AI age.

THE AI-POWERED STRUCTURED INTERVIEW – STANDARDIZING EVALUATION FOR ENHANCED PREDICTABILITY

Building on the foundation of **automated psycho-metric assessments**, let's now move into the next phase of the **Selection Rater** process: the **Structured Interview**. This stage plays a critical role in transitioning from predictive data points to deeper, human-centered evaluation. And more importantly, it's an area where AI can add meaningful value—enhancing both the **efficiency** and **objectivity** of your hiring process without sacrificing the richness of personal interaction.

Structured interviews differ from traditional interviews in one key way: **consistency**. Rather than relying on informal conversations or spontaneous questions, structured interviews use a pre-defined set of questions that are asked in the same way, in the same order, to every candidate. These questions are designed to elicit specific behaviors, experiences, and competencies that align with the **Ideal Candidate Profile (ICP)** you've defined earlier in the process.

This systematic approach makes structured interviews uniquely well-suited for **AI integration**. Here's why:

- **Standardization enables automation.** Because the questions are consistent and the expected responses fall within recognizable patterns, AI can be trained to assist with scoring and evaluating candidate answers. Whether it's analyzing language, tone, or content, AI can provide real-time feedback, surface red flags, or identify alignment with key competencies.

- **Bias reduction.** AI-supported structured interviews help mitigate common human biases by ensuring all candidates are evaluated on the same criteria. While human intuition is still important, especially for assessing cultural fit, AI helps ensure the process is anchored in fairness and focused on the factors that truly predict success.

- **Enhanced documentation.** Structured interviews generate a rich data trail. AI can capture and analyze this data to create interview summaries, generate candidate scorecards, and highlight strengths and gaps. This saves recruiters time while supporting better hiring decisions based on comparable, repeatable data.

- **Scalability.** As hiring needs grow, structured interviews supported by AI allow you to maintain consistency across interviewers, departments, and locations. This means your selection process doesn't lose quality as it scales—something that's nearly impossible to guarantee in traditional, unstructured interviews.

And just as important: even with AI's support, structured interviews still preserve the human connection that makes interviews so powerful. You're not replacing human judgment, you're enhancing it. AI provides structure, insights, and data, but **you** make the call based on how well the candidate fits with your team, your culture, and your goals.

In the chapters ahead, we'll take a closer look at how to design effective structured interview questions, how to train AI to support this process responsibly, and how to interpret results in ways that go beyond the numbers to surface real human potential.

Understanding the Structured Interview: A Framework for Fair and Consistent Evaluation

Unlike unstructured interviews, which can feel more like informal conversations and often vary wildly from one interviewer to the next, **structured interviews** bring clarity, consistency, and a strong foundation of fairness to the hiring process. In a structured interview, each candidate applying for a specific role is asked the **same set of predetermined questions**, in the **same order**, and their responses are assessed using standardized scoring rubrics or benchmarks.

This methodical approach is more than just a formality. It's a proven strategy to elevate the quality of your hiring decisions and ensure every candidate has an equal opportunity to demonstrate their potential. Structured interviews aim to accomplish several key outcomes that traditional approaches often struggle to achieve:

1. Increase Fairness and Reduce Bias

One of the most important benefits of structured interviews is their ability to reduce subjectivity and **minimize interviewer bias**. By standardizing the questions and evaluation criteria, structured interviews ensure that candidates are assessed on the **same playing field**, regardless of their background, appearance, or the mood or preferences of the interviewer.

In unstructured interviews, biases—both conscious and unconscious—can creep in easily. Interviewers may make decisions based on rapport, intuition, or how similar a candidate feels to them. Structured interviews don't eliminate human bias entirely, but they provide a much-needed framework that helps keep the process **anchored in job-related factors** rather than gut feelings.

2. Improve Reliability and Validity

Reliability in hiring means that if two interviewers evaluated the same candidate using the same method, they'd arrive at similar conclusions. Validity means the interview actually measures what it's supposed to measure—namely, whether the candidate is likely to perform well in the role.

Structured interviews score higher on both counts.

By using a consistent question format and scoring rubric, you remove much of the noise that plagues unstructured interviews and end up with a process that's both repeatable and predictive. Research consistently shows that structured interviews are among the most valid predictors of future job performance, especially when paired with assessments or work sample tests.

3. Enable Better Comparison Between Candidates

One of the most frustrating parts of hiring is trying to compare candidates who were evaluated in totally different ways. Structured interviews solve this by giving you comparable data. When everyone is asked the same questions, and responses are scored using a standardized rubric, it becomes much easier to objectively assess who truly meets the requirements—and who doesn't.

Instead of relying on anecdotal impressions or scattered notes, structured interviews give you a clear, side-by-side view of how each candidate performed relative to the job's core needs.

4. Focus on Job-Relevant Competencies

Structured interviews are built around assessing the knowledge, skills, abilities, and other characteristics—commonly referred to as KSAs—that are directly tied to success in the role. This focus ensures that you're spending your limited interview time evaluating the *right* things.

These competencies are often derived from your Ideal Candidate Profile (ICP) and might include things like problem-solving ability, communication style, leadership potential, or technical knowledge. Instead of asking vague or irrelevant questions, you're zeroing in on the specific capabilities that matter most for performance in the role.

Structured interviews don't just make your process more rigorous—they make it **more human**, too. They give every candidate a fair shot to tell their story, provide clear expectations, and foster a sense of transparency that today's job seekers deeply appreciate.

In the next section, we'll explore how AI can be layered into this structure to help with scoring, consistency, and real-time feedback, further amplifying the impact of this powerful hiring tool.

AI's Role in Delivering and Evaluating Structured Interviews: Automation for Consistency and Insight

One of the greatest strengths of structured interviews is, ironically, what might seem like a limitation at first glance: their rigidity. But that very structure—the use of standardized questions, uniform evaluation criteria, and consistent delivery—makes them exceptionally well-suited for AI-powered delivery and evaluation.

Unlike free-flowing interviews that require a high degree of human judgment and improvisation, structured interviews can be systematized. This makes them an ideal match for the precision and consistency that AI brings to the table. Let's explore the three key ways AI can enhance this stage of your selection process:

Automated, Consistent Delivery

AI can fully automate the delivery of structured interviews, ensuring every candidate experiences the exact same process, down to the wording of the questions, the pacing, and the format. This not only reinforces fairness and consistency but also enables you to scale your interview process without sacrificing quality or personalization.

Depending on your needs, AI platforms can deliver interviews through:

- **Text-Based Chatbots:** Candidates interact with a conversational interface that presents each question in sequence. Responses are recorded and analyzed in real time or after completion.

- **Pre-Recorded Video Interviews:** Candidates respond to a fixed set of video-recorded questions. These responses can be evaluated asynchronously by AI (and/or humans), speeding up turnaround time and eliminating scheduling constraints.

- **Virtual Avatars or Interview Bots:** Some platforms go a step further, using AI-powered avatars that simulate human interaction, creating a more dynamic and engaging experience, especially helpful for roles that require verbal communication or presentation skills.

In all formats, AI ensures every applicant receives a **uniform interview experience**, reinforcing the principles of equity and structured evaluation.

Objective, Data-Driven Evaluation

After the interview is delivered, the next opportunity for AI lies in **scoring** and **analysis,** turning subjective impressions into measurable insights. AI can evaluate responses using a combination of sophisticated techniques, including:

- **Keyword Recognition:** AI scans responses for specific phrases, skills, or competencies that match your Ideal Candidate Profile (ICP). This ensures alignment with the core capabilities needed for the role.

- **Sentiment Analysis:** AI can evaluate tone and language to detect enthusiasm, positivity, hesitation, or confidence. This doesn't replace human interpretation, but it can highlight areas of interest or concern.

- **Natural Language Processing (NLP):** NLP algorithms analyze the structure, depth, and logic of responses. They can assess how well a candidate articulates their thoughts, demonstrates understanding, or works through a scenario, offering deeper insight into **problem-solving** and **critical thinking** skills.

- **Verbal and Non-Verbal Cue Analysis (in Video Interviews):** While still developing, AI is beginning to detect subtle behavioral cues like facial expressions, eye movement, body language, and vocal pitch. These inputs can provide additional context around a candidate's confidence, clarity, and communication style, though these indicators should always be interpreted carefully and ethically.

Together, these tools bring a level of **objectivity and consistency** that's difficult to achieve with human evaluators alone, particularly in high-volume or fast-paced hiring environments.

Fast, Structured Data Collection and Analysis

One of the most transformative advantages AI brings to the interview process is its ability to capture, organize, and analyze candidate data in real time. Rather than relying on handwritten notes, fragmented spreadsheets, or memory-based impressions, AI platforms automatically record and transcribe candidate responses, whether delivered via text, audio, or video. This creates a clean, structured dataset that's easy to review, compare, and share across your hiring team.

Once the data is captured, AI tools can generate summary reports that highlight each candidate's key strengths, developmental areas, and alignment with the specific competencies required for the role. These summaries are not only consistent—they're also deeply informative, giving you a clear sense of how each individual stacks up against your Ideal Candidate Profile (ICP).

In addition to individual analysis, AI can provide comparative metrics, helping you see how a candidate performs relative to others in the same hiring pool. These side-by-side comparisons are especially useful when making tough decisions between multiple strong contenders. They ensure that decisions are grounded in data, not just intuition, and that every candidate is evaluated using the same standardized criteria.

AI also supports collaborative decision-making by centralizing interview data and insights in one place. Hiring managers and recruiters can access structured reports, review transcripts, and see quantitative scoring in real time. This not only speeds up the decision process but also promotes transparency and alignment among everyone involved in the hire.

Together, these capabilities do more than streamline the hiring process—they elevate the quality of decision-making. When combined with earlier predictive assessments and a well-defined ICP, AI-powered data collection gives your hiring team the clarity and confidence needed to move quickly, act strategically, and secure top talent before competitors do.

The Bottom Line: Structure + AI = Scalable, Fair, and Insightful Hiring

By combining the built-in rigor of structured interviews with the analytical power of AI, you get a process that's scalable, equitable, and grounded in data, without losing the human touch. AI enhances speed, consistency, and insight, while structured interviews ensure you're asking the *right* questions in a fair and focused way.

The "Science" and "Art" of the AI-Powered Structured Interview

As noted previously, selection involves both "science" and "art." In structured interviews with AI:

- **The "Science" (50%)**: The structured interview questions development, ideal response definition, scoring rubrics, and algorithms used by AI to analyze responses represent the "science" aspect. This relies on job analysis data, competency models, and statistical validation to ensure questions are relevant and evaluations predictive of performance. AI's objective analysis further contributes to this stage's scientific rigor.

- **The "Art" (50%)**: While AI can automate delivery and initial evaluation, the human element remains crucial. Designing insightful behavioral and situational questions that effectively reveal past behavior (a strong predictor of future behavior) still requires human expertise. Additionally, interpreting nuanced responses and considering contextual factors may require human review, especially in borderline cases or when assessing less tangible qualities like cultural fit.

Benefits of Integrating AI into Structured Interviews

Incorporating AI into structured interviews brings a range of powerful advantages that can significantly enhance the hiring process. One of the most immediate and noticeable benefits is enhanced efficiency. AI can conduct interviews and analyze responses far more quickly than a human interviewer, enabling faster decision-making and reducing the time spent on early-stage assessments. This frees up recruiters and hiring managers to focus on higher-level tasks, like building relationships with top candidates and refining overall hiring strategy.

Another major advantage is the increased consistency and fairness AI brings to the interview process. Every candidate receives the same set of questions, delivered in the same way, and evaluated using the same criteria. This uniformity helps minimize the unconscious biases that can sometimes influence human-led interviews, promoting a more equitable experience for all applicants. In doing so, AI helps create a level playing field where candidates are judged purely on their responses, not on subjective impressions.

AI also enables a more data-driven approach to hiring. Rather than relying solely on handwritten notes or general impressions, recruiters gain access to structured analytics and detailed insights into each candidate's performance. AI can highlight strengths, flag areas for follow-up, and even predict potential role fit based on response patterns and competencies. This makes the selection process not only faster but also more accurate.

From a logistical standpoint, AI dramatically improves scalability. It can handle multiple interviews simultaneously without sacrificing quality or consistency. This is particularly valuable for organizations with high-volume hiring needs or tight recruitment timelines. Instead of bottlenecks and backlogs, you maintain a smooth, streamlined flow of candidates through the pipeline.

Finally, by automating the early stages of the structured interview process, AI allows recruiters and hiring managers to concentrate their time and energy where it matters most—on the most promising candidates. With AI handling the initial evaluations, you're free to delve deeper into specific areas of interest or concern during follow-up interviews, making your final assessments more informed and impactful.

In short, integrating AI into structured interviews doesn't just make hiring faster—it makes it fairer, more scalable, and more strategic, giving your organization a meaningful edge in identifying and securing top talent.

Navigating the Limitations: The Continued Need for Human Oversight

While the integration of AI into structured interviews offers clear and compelling advantages—efficiency, consistency, scalability—it's equally important to recognize its current limitations. AI is a powerful tool, but it isn't a full replacement for human intuition, empathy, or context-driven judgment. In fact, the most effective interview strategies strike a careful balance between automated support and human oversight.

One key limitation of AI is its lack of empathy and rapport-building ability. Unlike human interviewers, AI cannot pick up on emotional cues in the same nuanced way, nor can it establish a genuine sense of connection with candidates. This can be a disadvantage, particularly when trying to assess interpersonal skills or emotional intelligence—qualities that often emerge naturally through conversation and personal interaction. The absence of this human element can make AI-led interviews feel transactional, potentially affecting candidate experience and limiting the richness of insights gathered.

AI systems can also struggle with nuance. When candidates provide unexpected or ambiguous responses, a human interviewer might sense an opportunity to dig deeper, ask a follow-up question, or reframe the discussion. AI, on the other hand, is constrained by its programming and training—it may misinterpret these responses, overlook subtle indicators of strength or concern, or fail to adjust course mid-interview. This rigidity means that valuable information can sometimes be lost in translation.

Another critical factor to consider is AI's dependence on training data. The accuracy, fairness, and overall effectiveness of AI evaluation rely heavily on the quality and representativeness of the data on which it has been trained. If the training data is biased—whether along lines of gender, ethnicity, education, or experience—it can reinforce and even amplify those biases in candidate assessments. That's why continuous monitoring, auditing, and refinement of AI models are essential for ethical, equitable implementation.

Finally, while structured interviews are designed to assess competencies and job-relevant skills, they don't always capture the intangible but essential "fit" factor. Cultural alignment, team compatibility, and interpersonal chemistry often make the difference between a good hire and a great one. These dimensions are highly subjective and context-specific, and AI isn't yet capable of reliably evaluating them. Human oversight remains crucial for determining whether a candidate will truly thrive within your team and organizational culture.

In short, while AI can enhance structured interviews in powerful ways, its effectiveness is maximized when paired with thoughtful, experienced human judgment. By understanding where AI shines—and where it falls short—you can design a hiring process that's not only efficient and consistent but also empathetic, inclusive, and deeply human.

Conclusion: Leveraging AI to Enhance the Science of Interviewing

Integrating AI into your structured interview process offers a powerful way to enhance evaluation efficiency, consistency, and objectivity. By automating delivery and providing data-driven insights into candidate competencies, AI allows you and hiring managers to focus expertise on more nuanced, human-centric selection aspects, such as assessing fit and making final hiring decisions. The AI-powered structured interview represents a significant step toward a more scientific, predictive talent acquisition approach, ultimately helping you hire more high-quality candidates. Next, we'll explore the crucial role of the Fit Interview in adding the final layer of human judgment to the Selection Rater.

CHAPTER 8

THE FIT INTERVIEW – THE ESSENTIAL HUMAN TOUCH IN FINAL CANDIDATE EVALUATION

Following the automated efficiency of AI in sourcing, screening, and structured competency assessment, we arrive at the final Selection Rater stage: the Fit Interview. This chapter explores this more personal, subjective interview's critical role in evaluating a candidate's alignment with company culture, team dynamics, and hiring manager preferences. While AI streamlines earlier hiring process stages, the Fit Interview remains a domain where the human touch isn't just valuable but essential.

Understanding the Purpose of the Fit Interview: Beyond Skills and Qualifications

Unlike the structured interview, which is designed to assess specific skills and experiences against clearly defined criteria, the Fit Interview serves a different—but equally important—purpose in the hiring process. Rather than focusing on hard qualifications, this interview aims to evaluate the more subtle, human elements of a candidate's profile that often determine long-term success and satisfaction within a company.

One of the core objectives of the Fit Interview is assessing cultural fit. This means evaluating whether the candidate's values, work style, and personality align with the broader organizational culture. When there's a strong cultural match, employees tend to experience higher job satisfaction, collaborate more effectively, and stay with the company longer. It's about asking: Will this person thrive in the way we work and what we stand for?

Another important focus is team compatibility. Beyond fitting into the company as a whole, it's essential to consider how well the candidate is likely to mesh with the specific team they'd be joining. This involves looking at communication preferences, interpersonal dynamics, and the candidate's comfort level with the team's existing workflow. The goal is to build teams that don't just function, but function *well* together.

The Fit Interview also provides an opportunity to assess the potential relationship with the hiring manager. This includes gauging rapport, mutual expectations, and communication styles. A positive, trusting relationship between a manager and their direct report is one of the strongest predictors of long-term engagement and performance. It can influence everything from daily morale to long-term career development.

Finally, the Fit Interview allows you to explore the candidate's motivation and passion. Why are they interested in this role? What excites them about your company? Do they demonstrate curiosity, energy, and a willingness to grow? Passionate candidates often bring a level of commitment and resilience that can't be captured through résumés or assessments alone.

Together, these insights from the Fit Interview complement the more objective data gathered through structured interviews and assessments, ensuring that hiring decisions reflect not just *who can do the job*, but *who will truly thrive* in it.

Why AI Falls Short: The Subjectivity of "Fit"

While AI is incredibly effective at analyzing large volumes of data and identifying patterns based on objective criteria, evaluating "fit" remains one area where human judgment is not only valuable but essential. Fit is inherently subjective, rooted in interpersonal dynamics, emotional resonance, and subtle cues—factors that are difficult, if not impossible, for AI to fully capture at this stage of its development.

One major limitation is AI's lack of empathy and intuition. Assessing fit often relies on gut instinct, emotional intelligence, and the ability to read between the lines. Human interviewers can pick up on non-verbal cues like tone of voice, facial expressions, or moments of hesitation—elements that might signal enthusiasm, doubt, or underlying concerns. They can also ask thoughtful follow-up questions in the moment, adjusting the conversation to better understand the candidate's motivations, personality, and potential compatibility with the team.

Another challenge is the difficulty AI faces in quantifying culture. Company culture isn't a checklist—it's often intangible, shaped by shared values, informal norms, communication styles, and unwritten rules. While AI can analyze stated values or employee feedback, it struggles to fully grasp the lived experience of working within a specific organizational culture. That makes it difficult for algorithms to determine whether a candidate will truly thrive in that environment.

There's also the issue of contextual understanding. What makes someone a good fit for one team or manager might not translate to another, even within the same company. Cultural dynamics, leadership styles, team structures, and even project timelines can all influence whether a candidate is likely to succeed in a particular context. AI systems typically apply generalized models, which makes it difficult for them to tailor their assessments to these more nuanced, situational factors.

And finally, there's the elusive but very real "likeability" factor—that immediate sense of connection or natural rapport that sometimes happens during an interview. While not a metric you'll find in any algorithm, this element of human chemistry can often influence team harmony and long-term satisfaction. AI, for all its strengths, can't replicate that spark.

In short, while AI can support and inform the fit evaluation process, it can't replace the uniquely human abilities required to assess whether someone will truly belong, contribute, and flourish within a specific role, team, or culture.

The Role of the Human Interviewer: Adding the "Art" to Selection

Given AI's current limitations in evaluating interpersonal dynamics and cultural alignment, the Fit Interview remains firmly in the hands of a human interviewer—often you, the recruiter, or more commonly, the hiring manager. This stage is where your judgment, intuition, and people skills come into play in a way no algorithm can replicate. Your role here isn't just important—it's essential.

One of your first responsibilities is building rapport. A strong Fit Interview depends on creating a space where candidates feel comfortable being themselves. When candidates feel at ease, they're more likely to open up and share genuine thoughts about their values, preferences, and working style. This natural, unscripted conversation often reveals more about a person than any assessment ever could.

You'll also be asking open-ended questions—ones that invite stories, reflections, and personality to come through. Rather than asking for a list of strengths or accomplishments, you might ask about how they've handled conflict, what they value most in a team, or what kind of work environment brings out their best. These responses offer real insight into how they think and operate.

As you listen, you're also observing non-verbal cues. Body language, tone of voice, and facial expressions can tell you just as much as the words being spoken. Does the candidate light up when discussing a particular topic? Do they appear confident, thoughtful, reserved, or overly rehearsed? These small signals help paint a fuller picture of who they are.

The Fit Interview is also your opportunity to assess interpersonal skills. Can this person communicate clearly? Do they seem like someone who can collaborate effectively with others? Could they represent your organization well to clients or cross-functional teams? You're looking for indicators that suggest how they'll function within your unique team dynamic.

Equally important is gauging cultural alignment. You're listening not just for what they've done, but for what they believe in and how they approach their work. Do their values align with your organization's mission and vision? Are their priorities in sync with your company's guiding principles and ways of working?

And ultimately, you'll be making a subjective, experience-driven judgment—drawing on your own instincts, your understanding of the team, and your knowledge of the company's culture. No algorithm can tell you with certainty whether someone is the "right fit." That decision comes down to your insight as a recruiter or manager—insight that is irreplaceably human.

The Importance of the Fit Interview in Overall Hiring Success

While the Fit Interview may seem subjective compared to more structured assessments, its role in ensuring long-term hiring success is critical. In fact, fit often determines whether a great hire stays and thrives, or quietly disengages and eventually leaves. Even the most skilled, experienced candidate can struggle if they're placed in an environment where they simply don't feel aligned with the values, norms, or day-to-day dynamics of the team.

When a new hire isn't a strong cultural fit, it can lead to decreased job satisfaction. The individual may feel out of sync with how things are done or disconnected from the organization's purpose. Over time, this sense of misalignment can erode morale, reduce motivation, and affect overall engagement. They might be capable, but they're unlikely to feel fulfilled.

Misalignment can also result in team friction. A candidate who doesn't mesh with the team's communication style or collaborative approach may inadvertently disrupt workflow, create tension, or hinder productivity. This isn't about personal shortcomings—it's about fit. Even well-meaning, talented people can clash with established dynamics if they're not well-matched.

Perhaps most concerning is the impact on retention. Candidates who feel out of place are significantly more likely to leave within the first year, sometimes even within the first few months. This leads to costly turnover, requiring the company to restart the recruitment, onboarding, and training process, often at the expense of time, budget, and team momentum.

Finally, a pattern of hiring individuals who don't align with your organization's values can slowly begin to erode company culture. When people who operate outside the organization's core principles become embedded in teams, it can dilute or shift cultural norms, leading to inconsistency and confusion across the workforce.

In short, the Fit Interview is far more than a subjective formality—it's a strategic safeguard. When done well, it helps protect your culture, strengthen your teams, and ensure that new hires not only perform but truly belong.

Conclusion: Balancing Efficiency with the Essential Human Element

While AI has revolutionized many recruitment aspects, the Fit Interview remains a critical stage where human judgment and interpersonal skills are indispensable. By allowing you or hiring managers to personally assess a candidate's cultural fit, team compatibility, and overall alignment, you can make more informed hiring decisions that help build a cohesive, high-performing, engaged workforce. The Fit Interview ensures that while AI drives efficiency in early stages, the final decision incorporates the crucial human element necessary for long-term success and retention.

CHAPTER 9

THE FUTURE OF LEARNING AND DEVELOPMENT – AI-POWERED TRAINING AND COACHING

Building on the efficiency gains achieved through AI in sourcing, screening, selection, and scheduling, let's explore the next talent management frontier: automating training and coaching using artificial intelligence. While still in early stages, AI promises to revolutionize how organizations develop talent, offering personalized, scalable, continuously improving learning experiences.

The Current Landscape: Human-Led Training and Coaching

Traditionally, training and coaching have been human-centric processes. Training programs are typically developed and delivered by learning and development professionals, while coaching comes from managers or specialized coaches. These methods, while valuable, can be time-consuming, resource-intensive, and not always tailored to individual employee needs. Companies often struggle to identify which employees will truly benefit from training, leading to wasted resources and frustrated trainers and coaches dealing with individuals who may lack the inherent potential to improve.

The Inevitable Shift: Embracing AI in Learning and Development

The future of training and coaching is clearly moving toward AI-powered automation, and for good reason. Organizations are increasingly recognizing the potential of AI to not only scale learning programs but to personalize them in ways that traditional approaches simply can't match. Instead of offering one-size-fits-all training modules, AI can analyze each employee's unique skills, knowledge gaps, learning style, and career aspirations to craft a customized learning journey. This ensures that individuals receive the right content, at the right time, and at the right pace—maximizing both engagement and effectiveness.

AI also brings a new level of scalability and accessibility to training programs. Whether your team is in one office or spread across the globe, AI platforms can deliver consistent learning experiences to thousands of employees simultaneously. This eliminates geographical and logistical barriers, making high-quality training available to everyone, regardless of location, time zone, or schedule. For organizations of all sizes, this shift significantly reduces the cost and complexity of traditional learning and development models.

Perhaps one of the most powerful aspects of AI-driven training is its ability to generate data-driven insights. These systems can track employee progress in real time, identify where individuals are struggling, and highlight which content is most effective. For learning and development teams, this creates a feedback loop that enables constant improvement of training content and delivery strategy, ensuring the learning experience continues to evolve alongside employee needs and business goals.

Finally, AI enables just-in-time learning, embedding training and support directly into an employee's workflow. Need help navigating a new system or brushing up on a process? Intelligent chatbots or virtual assistants can deliver guidance on the spot, offer quick refreshers, or link to the most relevant resources. This real-time support keeps learning continuous, contextual, and immediately applicable, helping employees stay productive while they grow.

As AI continues to mature, its role in learning and development will only expand, making training more personalized, efficient, and impactful than ever before.

Generative AI: A Glimpse into Automated Development's Future

We're already beginning to see the early stages of the Generative AI revolutionizing learning and development. Best known for its ability to create original content—text, images, code, and more—Generative AI is now being tested as a powerful force in automating training and coaching at scale. While these applications are still emerging, the potential is vast, and the implications for how we train, coach, and support employees are profound.

One of the most exciting opportunities lies in automated content creation. Generative AI models can quickly produce training materials tailored to specific roles, skill levels, or learning styles. Imagine creating an entire onboarding program, complete with interactive modules, practice scenarios, and personalized assessments—in a fraction of the time it would take traditional teams to develop the same content. This doesn't just save time; it enables learning programs to evolve faster and respond more flexibly to business needs.

Beyond static content, AI-powered virtual coaches are on the horizon. These advanced systems could function as intelligent, always-available mentors, offering guidance, answering questions, and even walking employees through simulated workplace situations to build practical skills. Unlike basic chatbots, these virtual coaches could personalize their support based on an employee's performance data, learning history, and career trajectory, providing feedback that feels tailored and human-like.

Generative AI also opens the door to adaptive learning experiences, where training platforms respond in real time to how a learner is progressing. If a user is struggling with a concept, the system could automatically adjust the pace, provide extra explanations, or offer an alternative learning method. If a learner is excelling, the AI could fast-track them through foundational material and move them on to more advanced content.

This kind of responsiveness creates a more engaging, efficient, and effective learning environment.

While much of this technology is still developing, the direction is clear: Generative AI will play a central role in shaping the future of workforce development. The result is not just smarter training, but a new era of personalized, scalable, and continuously evolving learning experiences—bringing world-class development opportunities to every corner of the organization.

Addressing Challenges and Considerations

While the potential benefits of AI in training and coaching are impressive, it's equally important to acknowledge and address the challenges and considerations that come with its adoption. As with any transformative technology, thoughtful implementation is key to ensuring long-term effectiveness, ethical use, and employee trust.

One major consideration is preserving the human touch. Just as the Fit Interview in the selection process relies on human intuition and emotional connection, aspects of coaching, such as empathy, encouragement, and relationship building, are inherently human. AI can simulate certain aspects of conversation and provide intelligent feedback, but it still falls short in delivering the deep interpersonal nuance that a human coach offers. For this reason, a blended approach that combines AI-powered tools with human coaching interactions may be the most effective strategy, leveraging the strengths of both to support learning and development holistically.

Another critical area is data privacy and security. As AI systems collect and process sensitive employee information, ranging from skills assessments to behavioral patterns, organizations must take clear and proactive steps to safeguard that data. Transparent communication around what data is collected, how it's used, and who has access to it is essential for building employee confidence. Strong data protection protocols, compliance with legal standards, and ethical data governance must all be in place from the outset.

There's also the issue of algorithmic bias, which we've seen in recruitment tools and is just as relevant in training and coaching applications. If AI models are trained on skewed data, they may unintentionally reinforce existing inequalities, such as offering more development opportunities to certain groups while overlooking others. Organizations must actively monitor and audit their AI tools to ensure they are fair, inclusive, and equitable, offering all employees access to meaningful growth.

Finally, just like AI in selection requires regular validation, the same is true for AI-powered training and coaching. It's not enough to deploy these tools and assume they're working. Organizations must continually track outcomes and assess whether the AI is having a measurable, positive impact on employee performance, engagement, and retention. This feedback loop is essential for refining both the technology and the overall learning strategy.

In short, embracing AI in learning and development brings immense promise—but realizing that promise responsibly requires intentional design, ethical oversight, and ongoing evaluation. With the right safeguards in place, organizations can confidently move forward into a future where human potential is amplified, not replaced by intelligent technology.

Integrating AI into the Talent Development Ecosystem

Successfully integrating AI into training and coaching isn't something that happens by accident—it requires a clear, strategic approach that balances innovation with thoughtful implementation. To truly harness the power of AI, organizations need to go beyond simply adopting new tools. They must embed AI into the learning ecosystem in a way that aligns with their unique goals, challenges, and infrastructure.

The first step is to identify key areas where AI can add the most value. Not every element of training or coaching is equally suited for automation. The focus should be on tasks that are repetitive, data-driven, or that benefit from large-scale personalization—such as delivering content, tracking progress, and recommending learning paths. These are areas where AI can streamline workflows and enhance the learner experience without replacing the human elements that still matter most.

Once those areas are identified, organizations must invest in the right technologies. Choosing an AI platform isn't just about features—it's about fit. The tools you implement should align with your specific learning and development goals and integrate seamlessly with your existing HR and learning systems. Flexibility, scalability, and the ability to provide meaningful analytics are key considerations that ensure your tech stack can evolve alongside your organization's needs.

Equally important is preparing your people to succeed alongside the technology. That means upskilling your learning and development professionals so they can effectively design, manage, and optimize AI-powered learning experiences. When your L&D team understands how to leverage AI, they become strategic enablers—crafting programs that are not only tech-enhanced but also human-centered.

Finally, a successful rollout starts with piloting and iterating. Rather than launching AI across the board, start small with controlled pilot programs. Test how well your chosen tools perform, gather real-time feedback from learners, and use performance data to guide refinements. This agile, feedback-driven approach allows you to make informed adjustments and ensure that when you scale, you're doing so with confidence and clarity.

By following this structured approach, organizations position themselves to build smarter, more responsive learning systems—ones that truly prepare their workforce for the future.

Conclusion: Empowering Employees for Success in the AI Era

Automating training and coaching through AI represents a significant opportunity to enhance talent development efforts. By leveraging AI, you can create more personalized, scalable, and effective learning experiences that empower employees to reach their full potential, contribute to a high-performance culture, and drive organizational success in our evolving work world. While the human element remains vital, AI will increasingly become integral to how organizations invest in their most valuable asset: their people.

CHAPTER 10

THE CRITICAL ROLE OF VALIDATION – TRACKING AI'S IMPACT ON PERFORMANCE AND RETENTION

As AI increasingly permeates all talent acquisition stages—from attracting and sourcing to screening and initial selection—validation becomes absolutely critical. Let's explore why tracking and assessing AI's effectiveness in predicting performance and retention isn't just a best practice but a necessity for building a truly successful, responsible AI-powered hiring strategy.

The Promise and Pitfalls of AI in Prediction

AI's core promise in recruitment lies in efficiently processing vast data to identify and select the highest-potential candidates. AI algorithms can analyze resumes, social media profiles, and assessment data to predict which candidates will likely succeed in specific roles and remain with your organization.

However, relying solely on AI without rigorous validation can lead to several pitfalls:

- **Efficiency vs. Effectiveness**: While AI excels at quickly moving paper-qualified candidates through initial stages (efficiency), it doesn't automatically guarantee selecting high-quality candidates who'll perform well long-term (effectiveness). Without validation, you might hire more candidates, but not necessarily the best ones.

- **The "Black Box" Problem and Unintended Bias**: Machine learning algorithms learn from input data. If this data contains historical biases, AI can perpetuate and amplify these biases, leading to discriminatory hiring practices. Validation helps identify and mitigate such unintended biases for fair, equitable outcomes.

- **The Dynamic Nature of Work and Skills**: Skills and competencies required for success evolve over time. AI models trained on past data may not accurately predict future performance

if job demands change. Continuous validation ensures algorithms remain relevant and
predictive.

- **Over-Reliance on Surface-Level Data**:
  AI sourcing and screening tools often focus on
  keywords and surface-level resume and profile
  information. Without validation against actual
  performance data, these tools may overlook
  candidates with excellence potential whose
  profiles don't perfectly match algorithm criteria.

The Imperative of Validation: Ensuring Responsible AI

"Responsible AI" combines AI efficiency with predictive model effectiveness. Validation is a responsible AI
cornerstone in recruitment. It provides evidence for
determining whether AI tools truly contribute to hiring
more quality candidates who are diverse, engaged,
retained, and productive.

Key Aspects of a Robust Validation Strategy

Investing in robust validation for your AI hiring tools isn't just a compliance checkbox—it's a strategic decision that delivers real and measurable benefits across the organization. At the core, validation ensures that your AI systems are doing what they're intended to do: helping you identify and hire candidates who are not only qualified on paper but who are also more likely to become high performers and stay with your company over time. This directly improves the effectiveness of your hiring decisions, leading to stronger teams and better long-term outcomes.

There's also a clear financial upside. When your hiring process consistently brings in well-aligned, high-fit candidates, turnover decreases. That means fewer repeat job postings, fewer hours spent onboarding replacements, and less productivity lost due to poor performance or early exits. Over time, these savings can add up significantly, making validation not just smart but cost-effective.

In addition to cost reduction, validation enhances productivity across your hiring team. When AI tools are accurately filtering and prioritizing candidates, both recruiters and hiring managers can focus their time and energy on the most promising individuals—those who meet your organization's specific performance criteria. This leads to more impactful interviews, better candidate engagement, and ultimately, faster and more confident hiring decisions.

Validation also plays a crucial role in protecting your organization from legal and reputational risks. As AI becomes more embedded in the hiring process, there's growing scrutiny around fairness, transparency, and bias. By rigorously testing and validating your AI systems, you can identify and address any unintended biases in the algorithms, helping to ensure compliance with employment laws and reinforcing your organization's commitment to ethical, equitable hiring practices.

Finally, validation empowers you to make more data-driven decisions. Instead of relying on assumptions or vendor promises, you gain concrete evidence about what's working—and what's not. This insight allows you to refine your talent acquisition strategies, choose the right AI tools, and allocate resources more effectively.

In short, validation isn't just about minimizing risk—
it's about maximizing the value and impact of your
entire AI-driven hiring strategy.

Conclusion: Building Trust and Driving Results with Validated AI

As you increasingly adopt AI in recruitment, validation transforms AI from a mere efficiency tool into a
true hiring effectiveness driver. By diligently tracking
performance and retention, conducting rigorous validation studies, and continuously monitoring for bias,
you ensure your AI-powered recruitment strategies
are not just efficient but also responsible, leading to
high-quality talent selection, improved organizational
performance, and a stronger, more engaged workforce.
Without this validation commitment, AI's promise
to revolutionize talent acquisition risks remaining
unfulfilled, potentially leading to unintended negative
consequences.

CHAPTER 11

REALIZING THE REWARDS – THE TANGIBLE BENEFITS AND ROI OF AI-POWERED HIRING

Throughout our journey, we've explored how integrating Artificial Intelligence into your talent acquisition process offers transformative opportunities for candidates, recruiters, and your entire organization. Let's now consolidate the key benefits for each stakeholder and explore the significant Return on Investment (ROI) that AI-powered hiring can deliver.

Benefits for the Candidate

When thoughtfully implemented, AI doesn't just improve internal efficiency—it also significantly enhances the candidate experience. From the moment a job seeker interacts with your company, AI-powered tools can create a smoother, more responsive, and more personalized journey for many candidates, which starts with an AI chatbot. These virtual assistants are available 24/7 to answer basic questions, provide clarity about the role, and guide applicants through the early stages of the process. It's an immediate touch-point that keeps candidates engaged, informed, and confident that their interest is being taken seriously.

What's more, the experience becomes increasingly personalized. AI-driven systems can tailor communications based on a candidate's profile, interests, and interactions. Instead of generic messages, applicants receive relevant information and nudges aligned with the specific roles they've applied for or expressed interest in. This sense of individual attention—delivered at scale—is something most traditional recruiting systems simply can't match.

Speed is another major benefit. By automating steps like sourcing, screening, and interview scheduling, AI dramatically shortens the time between application and meaningful engagement. Candidates no longer wait weeks just to hear if they've moved to the next step. This matters because research shows that 72% of candidates lose interest if they don't hear back within 10 business days. AI keeps the process moving, and candidates stay engaged.

Even for those who don't land the job, AI can still provide real value. Some platforms now offer career management insights based on candidate assessments, helping applicants better understand their strengths, skills, and ideal career paths. This turns the hiring process into a positive learning experience, even if it doesn't lead to an immediate offer, and leaves candidates with a lasting, favorable impression of your brand.

In a competitive talent market, this kind of thoughtful, AI-enhanced experience can be the difference between losing top talent and building lasting relationships with high-potential candidates.

Benefits for You as a Recruiter

For you as a recruiter, the introduction of AI into the hiring process can be a true game-changer. One of the most immediate and noticeable benefits is the relief from time-consuming administrative tasks. AI takes on the heavy lifting when it comes to high-volume candidate screening, quickly filtering out unqualified applicants based on your predefined criteria. This means you spend far less time digging through résumés that don't meet the mark and much more time engaging with high-potential candidates who are actually worth your energy.

AI also enhances the quality of the insights you have at your fingertips. Rather than relying solely on résumés or gut instinct, you're supported by data—smart algorithms that surface assessment results, identify behavioral patterns, and provide context around candidate strengths. This deeper understanding empowers you to more effectively "sell" career opportunities to top candidates, tailoring your messaging in ways that resonate with what each person values most.

Even the logistical headaches of scheduling interviews become a thing of the past. With AI-powered automation tools, the back-and-forth emails and calendar coordination are handled instantly. You get to focus on having meaningful conversations, not managing calendars.

Perhaps most importantly, by spending your time on better-qualified candidates and fewer dead ends, your day-to-day experience improves significantly. Recruiters often face burnout not from too much work, but from too much *ineffective* work. AI changes that. With a smarter, more strategic workflow, you'll feel more in control, less stressed, and more confident that your efforts are driving real results for both your organization and the people you help bring into it.

Benefits for Your Organization (ROI)

The most substantial impact of AI-powered hiring emerges at the organizational level, where it delivers a strong and measurable return on investment (ROI) across multiple dimensions. One of the most immediate benefits is the reduction in repetitive tasks. By automating sourcing, screening, and initial candidate engagement, AI frees up your HR and recruiting teams to focus on more strategic work, like candidate relationship-building, workforce planning, and refining employer branding. This shift not only boosts efficiency but also elevates the role of recruiters within the business.

Organizations that leverage AI in their early recruitment stages often see dramatically faster time-to-interview, as much as ten times faster, by automating candidate identification and first-touch engagement. Beyond speed, AI also helps to dramatically improve the quality of your talent pipeline. By aligning AI tools with a well-defined Ideal Candidate Profile (ICP), companies can increase the flow of quality candidates by up to 300%, ensuring that recruiters are engaging with individuals who are far more likely to succeed.

Timely, personalized engagement powered by AI also contributes to a smoother candidate experience, leading to significantly lower drop-off rates. When candidates feel seen and responded to early in the process, they're more likely to stay engaged, even in competitive job markets. Meanwhile, AI-assisted screening and selection processes—especially those incorporating validated, predictive assessments—help focus attention on candidates with high performance potential. This ensures that hiring decisions are based not just on qualifications, but on deeper indicators of future success and retention.

Better hiring decisions naturally lead to better retention outcomes. When you consistently hire candidates who are both highly capable and a strong fit for your organization's culture, you're not just retaining employees—you're retaining the *right* employees. These high performers, once in place, tend to attract and refer others like them, creating a self-reinforcing cycle that gradually builds a high-performance culture.

Conclusion: Embracing the Future of Hiring with AI

The evidence is clear: AI is no longer some distant, sci-fi dream—it's here, and it's already delivering real, measurable impact across the entire hiring ecosystem. From the way we identify and attract candidates to how we engage, evaluate, and retain top talent, AI is reshaping recruitment in ways that are both practical and transformative.

This isn't about replacing the recruiter—it's about **empowering** you. When used strategically, AI becomes an extension of your capabilities. It helps you engage candidates more effectively, reduces time spent on repetitive tasks, and delivers deeper insights that inform better hiring decisions. It frees you up to focus on what really matters: building relationships, crafting strategy, and aligning the right people with the right opportunities.

The return on investment can be substantial—not just in terms of time and cost savings, but in stronger hires, improved retention, and a more agile, resilient workforce. Organizations that embrace AI thoughtfully often see dramatic improvements in quality-of-hire, time-to-fill, and candidate satisfaction.

But here's the key: responsible implementation matters. To unlock AI's full potential, it's not enough to plug in the latest tools and hope for the best. Shiny software won't fix broken systems, and automation won't save a flawed strategy. You need to root your AI approach in responsible, people-first principles. That means prioritizing fairness, transparency, and accountability from day one. It means using data with integrity, validating outcomes regularly, and never letting convenience override ethics.

Responsible AI isn't just a checkbox—it's a mindset. It's the discipline to ask tough questions: Is this tool reducing bias or reinforcing it? Is our process inclusive? Are we measuring what actually matters, or just what's easy to track? It's about building a feedback loop that improves over time—auditing outcomes, training your team, and staying curious about what's working and what's not. Most importantly, it's about ensuring that your technology serves your people, not the other way around. When you get that right, you build trust not only with your candidates but with your entire organization.

Done right, AI doesn't just make you faster—it makes you sharper. It gives you a strategic edge. It helps you spot trends sooner, make better predictions, and elevate every stage of the hiring journey. It frees you up to lead.

And that's where the real transformation happens. So welcome to the future of recruitment—where technology amplifies your intuition, data supports your decisions, and you evolve into a next-generation hiring leader.

Again and again, AI can tell you a lot about a candidate's history, behaviors, and even likely performance patterns—but it can't change a candidate's DNA. And by DNA, we're talking about the core wiring: their drive, resilience, adaptability, and innate potential. Performance can be coached, improved, and optimized—but only within the bounds of that individual's raw capacity. AI can help you spot high-potential candidates more efficiently, but it can't manufacture grit, emotional intelligence, or ambition. That's why great recruiters don't just look at what someone *has* done—they look at what someone *can* do, and whether their natural wiring matches the demands of the role. The best hires happen when AI helps you spot potential, but your human judgment discerns if that potential can turn into high, sustainable performance.

Welcome to the era of the *AI Super Recruiter*. And yes—you're it.

CHAPTER 12

CONCLUSION – RESPONSIBLE AI

Efficiency X Effectiveness

The objective of this book was to provide a roadway to navigate the new landscape of AI-enabled recruiting. Implementing responsible AI and maximizing the efficiency of AI with the effectiveness of a validated predictor of performance requires the partnership of AI with the expertise of a Super Recruiter. The new Super Recruiter uses AI as a virtual assistant not only to increase efficiency but also to change the role from a reactive administrative processor to a strategic partner. We have explained in detail the benefits and limitations of AI at each stage of the talent acquisition process. The implementation of AI can be expensive if it is strictly efficient and not effective. Being attractive as an investment requires an understanding of ROI, which is an increase in performance and retention.

The following schematic summarizes the potential implementation of AI into a "responsible AI" process.

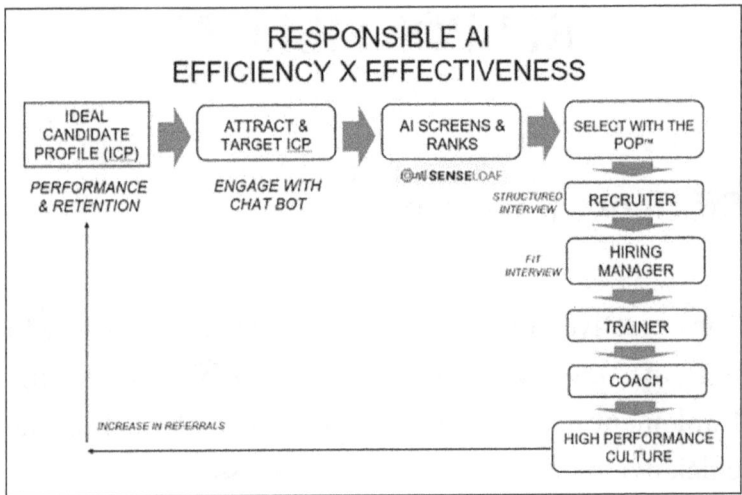

RESPONSIBLE AI
EFFICIENCY X EFFECTIVENESS

As outlined in detail, the anchor of a responsible AI process is the Ideal Candidate Profile (ICP, which is ideally based on performance and retention. Creating the ICP requires tracking the performance and retention of both new hires and existing employees and determining through a predictive study the characteristics that differentiate between high and low performers as well as the candidates that stay and leave. Also, when they leave. Early turnover is typically a screening or selection problem, whereas intermediate stages of turnover are typically onboarding and training issues.

Late-term turnover is more about mismatching the candidate with the coach, team, and/or culture.

The ICP is the basic formula for loading the algorithm of all sourcing strategies. For automated strategies like Indeed, career boards, etc., the ICP helps create job postings that target and appeal to candidates who match the career requirements well. The AI algorithm can load the predictive screening criteria to maximize the effectiveness of the initial screening and, through machine learning based on continuous validation, improve its predictive power by adding constructs or changing the weighting of the existing constructs. In terms of warm source recruiting, the ICP can be used to educate both nominators and centers of Influence on the type of candidates a specific organization is targeting. An important feature of an ATS like Talent Nest is tracking the number of quality candidates that are being attracted to the organization. This allows a recruiter to allocate the most resources to other sources that are attracting the most high-quality candidates. The recruiter then has the information to sell or justify the investment in a specific strategy to a CFO and the strategic business leader.

The ICP can also educate the chat bot on engagement strategies. Knowing the characteristics of top performers and the components of the ideal career path for a specific candidate can not only engage the candidate but also begin the process of selling the career. This would reduce the drop off rate of potential top performers. The more attractive the career opportunity and the sooner it occurs in the process, the less likely a high-quality candidate will drop off or accept another opportunity before learning more about the presented opportunity.

An AI screening process like Senseloaf is the first step toward the effectiveness journey. Loading the ICP onto their algorithm has allowed them to screen out low-potential candidates and also provide a ranking of candidates to save time and money on the selection process. In other words, the handoff to the psychometric assessment starts with the highest-ranked candidates. This is particularly effective when there is a quantity requirement within a specific time frame. For example, recruiting for a training class that begins the next month. The selection process can start with the highest-ranked candidates and continue until the number required by the class is achieved. It should be emphasized that the screening process is the green light to begin the selection process, not the hiring process. This is another benefit of AI screening algorithms: there is no chemistry to interfere with compliance with the process. We have found that when a recruiter likes a candidate, they often stop asking questions that might knock out a candidate. This, of course, creates a major problem with validation. To be predictive, a system must be consistent. Noncompliance or omitting steps in a process can confuse the model. Also, our data clearly shows that a consistent system outpredicts a non-compliant process.

Now, in the ideal model, only quality candidates are passed on to the automated psychometric assessment, which is the most predictive component of the selection process. As indicated in this book, we are now looking for the highest quality pieces of gold or the BEST candidates. The POP assessment predicts potential, along with training, coaching, and experience performance. It is now obvious the reason the ICP must be based on performance and retention; otherwise, this step becomes a simple descriptive step rather than a predictive step, and the recruiter will be required to further screen low potential candidates and continue with the remaining steps of the Selection Rater thereby negating the entire efficiency of AI.

In progress is the development of AI platforms that will conduct and score the structured Interview and free up either the recruiter or hiring manager to conduct the Fit Interview. At this point in the process, if all the steps have been followed, the successful candidates all have the Talent and Habits to PERFORM in the new culture, and the only question remaining is the Fit component. The task of the recruiter or hiring manager is to assess Fit and can NOT make a bad decision in terms of Performance Potential. The ideal Fit interview attempts to assess chemistry and understand the reasons the recruiter likes a candidate. In other words, move it from the Heart to the Head, From gut feel to intuition. We recommend that at the end of the fit interview, you ask yourself questions like, " Would you be comfortable introducing this candidate to your top performer?" or " Introducing this candidate to your team?" Finally, rate your assessment on a 5-point scale: " 5 = Excellent Fit to 1= Poor Fit". This is a good data point for future validation and feedback on fit decisions.

Trainers and coaches will immediately notice and appreciate the Super Recruiter delivering Quality candidates rather than simply checking a box and handing off candidates. Quality candidates are engaged in the training process, learn new skills and knowledge quickly, and continually seek out opportunities to maximize their performance potential. As highlighted in the Performance Equation, Quality candidates will also have the Talent and the Work ethic to maximize the ROI of coaching time and resources. Adding high-quality candidates to an existing high-performing team and culture creates a complementary synergy and exponential growth in team performance.

The final benefit and perhaps the most overlooked is the potential for referrals and warm source recruiting. Everyone in the community and workforce look up to successful individuals and want to know what they do and where they work. Most top Potential Performers want to join successful, winning teams.

In conclusion, the power and efficiency of AI is unlimited and will continue to grow at unprecedented rates. If this growth is at the expense of Effectiveness, it can create problems rather than be an effective solution. AI must be held accountable through continual validation to ensure that it predicts performance and retention and complies with all legal and ethical requirements. The Super Recruiter leverages AI but also holds it accountable through validation and providing the checks and balances to direct AI on what is predicting as well as what not to load on the predictive algorithms. Responsible AI is a balance of Efficiency and effectiveness. The Super Recruiter maximizes both Efficiency and Effectiveness and Unleashes AI and the power of a validated Predictor of Sales Performance.

Authors note: Thank you for reading my book. I enjoy feedback and sharing new ideas and concepts. If you would like to discuss any ideas generated through reading this book, or you are thinking about implementing AI or would like to sell Talent Nest AI or the POP, contact me directly atjmarshall@selfmgmt.com

www.ingramcontent.com/pod-product-compliance
Lightning Source LLC
Chambersburg PA
CBHW021930190326
41519CB00009B/974